L U C K

THE BRILLIANT RANDOMNESS

OF EVERYDAY LIFE

L U C K

THE BRILLIANT RANDOMNESS
OF EVERYDAY LIFE

N I C H O L A S

R E S C H E R

F A R R A R   S T R A U S   G I R O U X

N E W   Y O R K

LIBRARY OF CONGRESS CATALOGING-IN-PUBLICATION DATA
Rescher, Nicholas.
Luck : the brilliant randomness of everyday life / Nicholas
Rescher. — 1st ed.
p.   cm.
Includes bibliographical references.
1. Chance. 2. Fortune. 3. Fate and fatalism. I. Title.
BD595.R47 1995 123'.3—dc20 95-17421 CIP

FOR DOROTHY,
MY OWN BIT OF GOOD LUCK

CONTENTS

ACKNOWLEDGMENTS

This book has its origins in my 1989 Presidential Address to the American Philosophical Association on the topic of luck. My interest in these issues of philosophical anthropology has expressed itself in a series of publications reaching back to the 1960s, and the present book can be seen in this context as part of an ongoing effort at a philosophical scrutiny of the human condition in a complex and uncertain world.

I am indebted to my literary agent, Jim Hornfischer, for convincing me that the theme of luck deserved to be treated at book length. Richard Gale has enabled me to profit from his comments on a draft version of the manuscript. John Glusman offered many constructive editorial suggestions. John Williams helped with ideas for the iconography. I extend my thanks to them. And I am grateful to my secretary, Estelle Burris, for her patient help in turning my hen scratches into an elegantly word-processed text.

Pittsburgh, Pennsylvania
January 1995

L U C K

THE BRILLIANT RANDOMNESS
OF EVERYDAY LIFE

I N T R O D U C T I O N

1. LUCK AND THE HUMAN CONDITION

In the early morning hours of August 9, 1945, the B-29 *Bock's Car* bomber left the American airfield on Tinian island in the Pacific bound for the arsenal city of Kokura on the northern tip of Japan's Kyushu island. In the plane's belly sat "Fat Man," the second atomic bomb readied for military use. It was a plutonium-based implosion device with the explosive power of some thirteen thousand tons of TNT. Three days earlier, the bomber *Enola Gay* had dropped on Hiroshima the first such weapon, "Little Boy"—a bomb constructed on rather different, less sophisticated principles. And now phase two of the world's greatest physics experiment was about to take place. But matters did not go exactly as intended.

Over Kokura there was considerable cloud cover and haze, and the aiming point was obscured. In consequence, Army Air Corps Major Charles W. Sweeney proceeded southward as per contingency plan to the secondary target, the old port city of Nagasaki. There, Fat Man detonated, producing a ball of fire described by observers as twenty times brighter than sunlight. The rest, as the saying goes, is history. Kokura was a city literally saved by the clouds. And what was an incredible piece of good luck for the inhabitants of Kokura turned equally bad for those of Nagasaki.[1]

Luck need not, of course, make its impact so dramatically. On a lesser scale it is a reality that makes itself felt in every aspect of daily life. But it is a challenge to philosophers as well. Why is it a fact of life? What does it mean for the human condition? Why is life so unfair? And what should the moralist make of luck's destabilizing the balance between fate and merit? Such questions are obviously intriguing. And yet, since classical antiquity at any rate, philosophers have not taken luck as seriously as the topic demands.

The human significance of luck stems from the fact that it is one of the characteristic factors that define our condition. For while we are intelligent agents who make our way by thought along the pathways of a difficult world, we are agents of *limited* knowledge who do and must make our decisions in the light of incomplete information. And for this reason we are inevitably at the mercy of luck. Our choices and decisions propose, but the ultimate disposition is at the mercy of a force beyond the limits of our cognitive and practical control. When matters do indeed turn out as we design, then—all too frequently—it is by good luck rather than rationally determinative planning and execution. And if things go badly, then—all too frequently—it is by bad luck rather than sheer incompetence.

To be sure, once we intelligent creatures appear in this world under the aegis of evolution, it transpires that the world's eventuations must—normally and in general—be such that the bulk of what happens to us is in line with our sensible expectations. Most of what happens to the intelligent beings who have a thought-guided lifestyle on nature's stage must run as expected, and only a fraction of what substantially affects us can eventuate counter-expectedly. Were this not so, then creatures of *our* sort would not have developed and endured. But this of course does not mean that things will always go as we expect.

In matters of benefit, intelligent creatures find themselves in a

4

situation where there are two ways to lose out: actually suffering losses and not sustaining gains. Accordingly, our expectations can go wrong in two ways: (1) we expect something bad, but what actually happens is good (happy surprises); (2) we expect something good, but what actually happens is bad (disappointments). Here luck operates on both sides of the balance. The course of natural and rational selection at work in producing a viable community of rational creatures will presumably be such that happy surprises will have to outnumber disappointments. For since disappointments are physically and psychologically dangerous, and happy surprises are unproblematic (and indeed positive), evolutionary selective processes will so operate as to favor a prudence that produces substantially more favorable misjudgments (happy surprises) than unfavorable ones (disappointments). On this basis, good luck seems destined to outweigh the bad.

But good luck does not have the field to itself. Bad luck too exists and even has its uses. For when things go wrong, it is far more comforting and ego-protective to avoid an acknowledgment of personal fault by blaming one's bad luck. Luck is a most useful instrument of self-exculpation. One's self-image—and public image to boot—is obviously safeguarded whenever one can manage to avert personal culpability by deflecting blame for one's failures on uncooperative chance. (But of course in taking this stance, one is also less likely to profit by the useful lessons that such experiences afford.)

Interestingly enough, the domain of luck is not limited to this life alone. For one can also have posthumous luck to exactly the extent that one can have posthumous interests. It seems altogether plausible to say that it was unlucky for Christopher Columbus that the continent came to be called America, after the insignificant cartographer Amerigo Vespucci, instead of Columbia, after its actual discoverer. The long, long reach of luck extends even beyond the grave.

2. THE LANGUAGE OF LUCK

Luck as an English word is a creature of the fifteenth century and derives from the Middle High German *gelücke* (modern German *Glück*), which (somewhat unfortunately) means both happiness *and* good fortune, conditions that are certainly not necessarily identical. Virtually from its origin, the term has been applied particularly to good or ill fortune in gambling, in games of skill, or in chancy ventures generally.[2]

What is useful for the discussion of luck—and what several European languages do not make available—is a single word to mean "good or bad fortune acquired unwittingly, by accident or chance" ("ein zufälliges Glück oder Unglück"). In English, *luck* does exactly this job; in other languages we have to do the best we can.[3] For *luck* fares rather mixedly in European languages. The Greek *tuchê* is too much on the side of haphazard. In Latin, *fortuna* comes close to its meaning, with the right mixture of chance (*casus*) and benefit (be it positive or negative). But the German (as indicated) suffers from the unfortunate equivocation that *Glück* means not only *luck* (*fortuna*) but also *happiness* (*felicitas*). The French *chance* (from the Latin *cadere*, meaning how matters fall—"how the dice fall") is a fairly close equivalent of *luck*, however. And the Spanish *suerte* is also right on target.

On the other side of the coin, several languages have a convenient one-word expression for "a piece of bad luck" (French *malchance*,

6

German *Pech*)—a most useful resource considering the nature of things, which English unaccountably lacks. (Despite its promising etymology, *misfortune* is not quite the same, since it embraces any sort of mishap, not merely those due to impredictable accident or chance but also those due to one's own folly or to the malignity of others.) And it may be emblematic of something larger that no European language seems to have a single-word expression for "a piece of good luck."

We may, from time to time, realize a wholly unanticipated boon. When such an event occurs, we are lucky indeed. But this happens to some more than to others. Good luck seems to accompany some people and bad luck to haunt others in a more or less systematic way. In English we do not have a special expression for such people—unlike German, where someone so favored can be called a *Glückskind* (child of good luck),[4] and someone not favored an *Unglücksrabe* (bad-luck raven). But while English lacks a convenient terminology to implement the distinction for those more or less systematically endowed with good (or bad) luck, we do have the expression *jinx* for someone who *brings* bad luck—though, curiously enough, no comparable expression for someone who brings us good luck.

Is the term *luck* strictly and literally applicable outside the human realm? It is clear that when we say the tree was lucky to escape uprooting in the hurricane, we speak figuratively. Does this mean that cats and dogs cannot be lucky? Not at all! Perhaps cats and dogs cannot *appreciate* their luck—cannot realize that they are lucky. But that, of course, does not mean that they cannot actually be lucky. (Cats and dogs presumably cannot realize that they are overweight, but that does not preclude them from being so.) There is no question that animals have interests and desires that can be affected by developments running contrary to any reasonable expectation that could be formed—not, of course, by them; that is actually immaterial, for here an intelligent spectator will do. The crux is that we can do it on their behalf; after all, it is *we* who characterize them as lucky. (One can be lucky without realizing it, even as one can be foolish without realizing it.) Luck pivots on having things go well or ill fortuitously from the angle of its beneficiaries. And as far as the nature of the recipient is concerned, the pivotal question is, once again, not "Can they reason?" but "Can they suffer?" And the fact that we ourselves can make judgments on the beneficiary's behalf serves to keep cats and dogs in the picture.

3. THE ICONOGRAPHY OF LUCK: THE DOMAIN OF FORTUNA

Many cultural phenomena attest luck's prominence on the human scene. Consider folklore and myth, for example. Fate and fortune— inexorable destiny and mere chance—have ever been close allies. The ancients associated the Greek goddess Necessity (*Anagkê, Necessitas*) with Fortune (*Fortuna*), a Roman goddess (of Etruscan or even earlier origin). Thus Horace (*Odes*, I, 35) portrayed Necessity as a forerunner and associate of Fortune, grasping in her brazen hands great nails, a clamp, and molten lead as symbols of tenacity and inflexibility. Usually, however, Necessity was depicted holding in her lap a spindle around which the world revolves, symbolizing the preordainedly stable rotation of the fixed stars; while here, in this imperfect, earthy domain, there was a greater scope for chance and accident, so that Fortune found more opportunity for her activities.[5]

However, Fortuna was also often linked to the Greek goddess Tychê, who was more closely associated with chance than with destiny. And so while the Romans at first thought of *fortuna* in terms of personal fate and fortune (and so as allied to Necessity), they eventually identified it with *fors*—chance, luck, happenstance, accident.

In this amalgamated Greco-Roman version, Fortuna was worshiped throughout the Roman Empire, and Pliny stated that in his day she was invoked in all places at every hour.[6] For Fortuna accordingly became a goddess with her own cult and numerous temples (one on the Tiber just outside the city). Early in the third century B.C., a colossal bronze statue of the goddess Tychê (Fortuna) as civic deity was erected in Antioch by Eutychides, a pupil of Lysippus. It was a majestic figure, seated on a rock and holding in her right hand ears of corn, which symbolized plentiful generosity, a godlike youth, representing the river Orontes (on which the town is sited), swam forth from between her feet. (A small marble statue in the Vatican and a silver statuette in the British Museum are supposed to be modeled on this original.[7])

Fortuna was deemed to be the firstborn daughter of Jupiter and a prime personage among the gods. She was frequently portrayed on Roman coins and carvings with a cornucopia, as the bestower of prosperity,[8] and a rudder, as the controller of destinies. The common practice of devotion and offerings to the goddess centered on the idea of securing her favor in averting evils and providing goods. Frequently, she was depicted with a wheel or even standing on a sphere to indicate the volatility and uncertainty of life's ups and downs. In various instances, the priestesses in temples to Fortuna operated an oracle that gave its responses through the outcome of die-tosses or the drawing of lots on which messages were inscribed (as with Chinese fortune cookies). Thus the association between Fortuna and games of chance goes back virtually to ancient Greece.

A coin of the reign of the emperor Vespasian depicts the Fortuna of the house of Augustus with her right hand resting on a rudder and her left hand holding a cornucopia. She stands on a wheel placed upon a small sphere.[9] This coin and others like it present the whole iconography associated with the goddess Fortuna in one compact package![10] Romans often had household statues to their own familial Fortuna as one of the Penates (household gods) of the house. And sometimes the goddess was painted at the entrance-door to houses. Now, that Fortuna should be seen as divine in antiquity is plausible enough, considering the powerful role of luck in human affairs. But why a divine *female*? Largely, no doubt, because of her role as nourisher and sustainer, symbolized by the gifts coming to us from that cornucopia. But partly also, apparently, because this would seem in line with the somewhat inconstant, fickle, and unpredictable way in which fortune bestows its favors upon mortals. Then, too, there are other connections. For in ancient times Fortuna was cultivated especially by women eager to improve their prospects in childbirth and to learn of the fortunes of their children. Many temples were dedicated to *Fortuna muliebris*, the woman's Fortuna,[11] with whom maidens interceded on behalf of future children and mothers on behalf of their actual ones. And so people envision "Lady Luck" as a helper down to the present day.

Another important way of representing luck arises in connection with games of chance. After all, the analogy of human life and games of chance also dates from classical antiquity, with Fortuna regarded as governing both the unfolding of human destinies and the outcome in matters of gaming and gambling. In the Middle Ages, certain games were specifically devised to exploit this analogy—the Game of Life, in particular, and also Chutes (or Snakes) and Ladders. In both these games, which are still played today, chance determines the progress or regress of an individual toward the attainment of ultimate success. In such games we have the characteristic mixture of chance and gain/luck represented in the design of a playing board that graphically depicts the impact of luck on human affairs.

Yet another sector of the Roman iconography of luck relates to the wheel of fortune (*rota fortunae*), which became one of the most popular and widely diffused secular icons of the Middle Ages.[12] It was commonly depicted as a great wheel on the order of a mill wheel, ridden by people, some on the way up, others on the way down, some "on top of the world," others "hitting bottom."[13] About the year 1100, Bishop Balderic of Dol, in Brittany, visited the Benedictine abbey at Fécamp, in Normandy, where he saw a large wooden wheel whose significance he did not at first comprehend:

Then, in the same church, I saw a wheel, which by some means unknown to me descended and ascended, rotating continually. At first I took this wheel to be an empty thing, until reason recalled me from the interpretation. I knew from this evidence of the ancient Fathers that the wheel of Fortune—which is an enemy of all mankind throughout the ages—hurls us many times into the depths; again, false deceiver that she is, she promises to raise us to the extreme heights, but then she turns in a circle, that we should beware the wild whirling of fortune, nor trust the instability of that happy-seeming and evilly seductive wheel: concerning these things those wise, ancient doctors have not left us uninstructed. By revealing these things, they have brought us to understanding.[14]

11

Luck was then pictured as a controlling agency determining willy-nilly people's place in the scheme of things, with our personal destinies under its ultimate control.

It is in a way ironic that Luck (*Fortuna*) and Necessity (*Anagkê*) were seen as allies and companions from antiquity onward. For they are in fact opposites—the one geared to blind and unpredictable chance, the other to foreordained and inexorable fate. The linkage doubtless roots in the human penchant for seeing Reason at work everywhere and for being unwilling to accent as mere random happenstance the things that are of fateful import for ourselves. (This tendency to see divine planning at work in the eventuations of apparent chance is clearly manifest in the use of sortilege for decision-making from classical antiquity onward.)

4. LUCK'S LONG REACH

In this life there is always the possibility of unforeseeable developments by which we stand to gain or lose. And the role of chance in human affairs is such that no matter which of the world's apparent goods we yearn for—be it money, power, prestige, or whatever—we will be at the mercy of luck.

Luck is a rogue force that prevents human life from being fully domesticated to rational management. Its foothold on the world stage is secure by the power of chance, chaos, and choice. Luck and her cousins, fate and fortune, make it somewhere between difficult and impossible to manage our lives successfully simply through planning and design. Things in this world can always take an unexpected turn; as the quip has it, "Life is what happens when you're not making plans." It was a commonplace among the ancient Greeks that no man should be accounted fortunate until after his death. At any stage, disaster may strike to upset everything despite all our best efforts and most careful contrivings. As John Dewey observed, our standing in the world's course of chances is ever risky:

> No one knows what a year or even a day may bring forth. The healthy become ill; the rich poor; the mighty are cast down; fame changes to obloquy. Men live at the mercy of forces they cannot control. Belief in fortune and luck, good and evil, is one of the most widespread and persistent of human beliefs. Chance has been defied by many peoples. Fate has been set up as an overlord to whom even the Gods must bow. Belief in a Goddess of Luck is in ill repute among pious folk but their belief in providence is a tribute to the fact no individual controls his own destiny.[15]

Considering the myriad ways in which luck makes its impact upon every human life, it is well worthwhile to have a closer look at what luck is and how it functions. As one nineteenth-century moralist reminds us, luck produces unexpected results: "The painter who produced an effect he had long toiled after in vain, by throwing his brush at the picture in a fit of rage and despair, the musical composer, who having exhausted his patience in attempts to imitate on the piano a storm at sea, accomplished the precise result by angrily extending his hands to the two extremities of the keys, and bringing them rapidly together,—all these seem to manifest some of the freaks of Fortune by which some men are enriched or made famous by their blunders, while others, with ten times the capacity and knowledge, are kept at the bottom of her wheel."[16]

The fact that human goods cover a wide spectrum many of whose components are more important than wealth—health and the fate of loved ones, for example—means that the poor are just as vulnerable to bad luck as the rich. Precisely because it bestows her favors on all manner of people, there is something decidedly democratic about luck. Fortune unquestionably favors capitalists over proletarians, but luck does not: it touches both the great people of this world and the small. Every sort of life admits of positive and negative developments, and the world's chanciness creates room for their impact upon all of us.

Seldom is luck—good and bad—more strikingly manifest than with an epidemic of a deadly disease. In his entry for July 25, 1832, the English diarist Charles Greville wrote:

> The dread of cholera absorbs everybody [in London]. Mrs. Smith, young and beautiful, was dressed to go to church on Sunday morning, when she was seized with the disorder, never had a chance of rallying, and died at eleven at night. This event, shocking enough in itself from its suddenness and the youth and beauty of the person, has created a terrible alarm; many people have taken flight, and others are suspended between their hopes of safety in country air and their dread of being removed from metropolitan aid.[17]

Its haphazard impact is one of the most frightening aspects of an epidemic of this nature, which selects its victims in a seemingly random way.

This chanciness is often strikingly manifested in a common characteristic of the biographies of "successful" people. Very few of them move in a straight line toward the career on which their fame and fortune rests. Early in life there is generally a period of being shuttled to and fro—an unsettled wandering among uncertain possibilities. But at last some fortuitous, seemingly random development sets their course in a direction from which there is no looking back. Some chance development—a random encounter or an unexpected opportunity—now impels them along a course which may seem inevitable to the wisdom of hindsight, but which, at the time, appeared to all concerned as little more than a piece of pure luck.

We are indeed fortunate to be born into the talents and advantages we have. But not lucky. It is not that our indeterminate protoself somehow won a lottery for a particular endowment. The life we come into is a matter of chance, but not of luck.

On the other hand, considering all of life's hazards, we are (most probably) lucky to be still alive—at any rate as long as we are able to enjoy an acceptable quality of life. And insofar as this is so, it is perfectly appropriate to say that "our luck runs out" when our earthly life is terminated. In fact, it is part of the human condition in this vale of tears that sooner or later our luck is bound to run out in this regard.

Sometimes our actual choices make no difference—it matters not which road we select when all the roads lead to Rome, so that the outcome is predetermined and inevitable. The result we attain is fixed quite independently of what we do about it; we are embarked on the ship, and no matter how we run about—or simply sit—the destination is foreordained. But life being what it is, this sort of situation is not very common. In general, what happens depends on what we do and on what others (including Mother Nature) contribute to the course of events. And insofar as those portentous outcomes depend on circumstances beyond our cognizance and control, the success of our own endeavors will be matters of luck.

Luck unquestionably deals very differently with different people. But, fortunately, there are also many different sorts of human goods—riches, intelligence, good looks, an amiable disposition, artistic talent, and so on. Mercifully, a person to whom circumstance deals a short suit in one department may well get a long suit in another: one can be unlucky at the gaming table of worldly fame and still be lucky in love. In a way, money is the most democratic of goods. In contrast to good looks or musical talent or a healthy constitution, one does not have to be born into money but can, with fortune's aid, acquire it as one goes along.

The happy-go-lucky individual downplays prudence and remains quite unconcerned about trying to ensure that things go well. She neither toils nor spins. Like the proverbial lily in the field, such a person lets the future look after itself, relying on luck—rather than prudent effort—to ensure that matters work out to the good. "By rights"—by the rules that standardly govern the world's course of events—things ought not to go all that well for such an individual. When they nevertheless do so—as does indeed occur—the happy-go-lucky person can be accounted lucky. Yet the fact remains that the individual for whom happy-go-lucky pays off is a lucky anomaly. Ordinarily it does not improve one's chances to leave matters to chance.

It is not just by having children that we become luck-subjected hostages to fortune, but by having a stake in anything whatsoever. Wherever we invest our hopes and aspirations—whatever may be our expectations and goals and plans—good or bad luck can come into operation to realize or disappoint our wishes and our needs. Our best-laid plans go awry for reasons entirely beyond our knowledge and control. Often systems designed to reduce the scope of luck in life end up increasing it. Falling victim to crime is clearly a piece of very hard luck. And as with crime so also with punishment. The crux of a rational system of criminal justice is to establish a just and sure linkage between the offense committed by wrongdoers and the punishment that comes upon them in virtue of such offenses. When this relationship breaks down, when actually suffering punishment for crimes becomes so rare as to fall into the category of bad luck—as seems to be the case in present-day America—then the system is rendered a mockery. It is ironic that a system instituted to ensure a due coordination between crime and punishment should leave the linkage at issue here as a matter of improbable chance, of mere bad luck.

Luck is the determiner of much of what happens to us in this world. Be we criminals or law-abiding citizens, we are, all of us, at the mercy of unpredictable developments that make it a matter of mere luck how many of the crucial issues of our lives are resolved. The fact is that most human enterprises are to some extent chancy. Effort alone is seldom sufficient because of all the things that could possibly go wrong: a mixture of effort and luck is often needed to achieve success. If we do not get "the breaks" in such a contingent venture, we may well fail despite doing all the right things. The common practice of wishing someone good luck is not a matter of suggesting that they are incompetent, but rather reflects our realization that competence alone is not enough to secure success in a chancy world—that there is always the prospect that even the best possible effort may not meet with the success it deserves.

Recognizing the prominent role of sheer luck throughout the realm of human affairs, this work will address such questions as: What is luck? How does it differ from fate and fortune? What should our attitude toward lucky and unlucky people be? Can we expect to control or master luck? Are people to be held responsible for their luck? Should there be compensation for bad luck? Can luck be eliminated in our lives? These questions and others like them set the agenda for these deliberations. For the philosopher, luck is a splendid theme because it brings together so many of the pivotal issues of the domain: chance and necessity, freedom and determinism, moral responsibility, historical inevitability, human finitude—the list goes on and on.

The main thesis of the book is that, like it or not, luck is an ineliminable part of the human condition. We could not exist as the sorts of creatures we are, and in our more buoyant moments are pleased and proud to be, if sheer dumb luck were not—for better or for worse—a major factor in our lives.

I

E N I G M A S O F C H A N C E

1. LUCK AND THE UNEXPECTED

We live in a world where our aims and goals, our "best-laid plans," and, indeed, our very lives are at the mercy of fortuitous chance and inscrutable contingency. In such a world, where we propose and fate disposes, where the outcomes of all too many of our actions depend on "circumstances beyond our control," luck is destined to play a leading role in the human drama.

As individuals, we may never know how lucky we actually are. With every step we take, chance can intervene for our good or ill. For all we know, we narrowly escape death a dozen times each day—failing to inhale a fatal microbe here, and there missing by a hair's breadth the pebble that would cause us to slip and pitch into an onrushing bus. Luck, then, is a formidable and ubiquitous factor in human life as we know it—a companion that, like it or not, accompanies us all from the cradle to the grave.

Luck is at work when things that are of significance to us occur fortuitously, by chance, as it were.[1] And "significance" here means that benefits or negativities must be involved. Sometimes, to be sure, a benefit can be assessed as such only in retrospect. Whether a marriage turns out well or not is something that will not be apparent on the wedding day. Accordingly, whether or not a man and woman are lucky to have found one another will be determinable only with the wisdom of hindsight. Generally, however, we judge goods and evils in the short run, without worrying about "how they will turn out in the end." (After all, as John Maynard Keynes observed, "in the long run we are all dead.")

Luck pivots on unpredictability. A world in which agents foresee everything according to a discernible plan leaves no room for luck. But we ourselves live in a very different sort of world. Things often go well or ill for us because of conditions and circumstances that lie wholly beyond our cognitive or manipulative control. It was a matter of bad luck for the Spain of King Philip II when a storm scattered the Invincible Armada in the English Channel. But it was a matter of good luck for Queen Elizabeth's subjects. Luck—good or ill— impinges upon individuals and groups alike (think of the Jews of Poland or the passengers on the *Titanic*). There is no way of escaping it in this world. We play our cards as best we can, but the outcome depends on what is done by the other players in the system—be they people or nature's forces. Our lives are lived amid hopes and apprehensions. Things can turn out for our weal or our woe in ways that we can neither foresee nor control. And it is exactly here that the factor of luck makes its inexorable way into the domain of human affairs. Often as not a person's life is a chain built up by links of luck. The youthful personal influences that inform one's career decisions, the contingencies that determine one's employment, the chance encounters that lead to one's marriage, etc., are so many instances of luck.

The role of chance in human affairs was once the topic of extensive discussion and intensive debate among philosophers. In Hellenistic Greece, theorists debated tirelessly about the role of *eimarmenê*, the unfathomable fate that remorselessly ruled the affairs of men and gods alike, regardless of their wishes and actions. The church fathers struggled mightily to combat the siren appeal of the ideas of chance and destiny—those superstition-inviting potencies. (Augustine detested the very word *fate*.) The issue of good or bad fortune, along with the related question of the extent to which we can control our destinies in this world, came to prominence again in the Renaissance, when scholars brooded once again about the issues of human destiny raised by Cicero and Augustine. And the topic undoubtedly has a long and lively future before it, since it is certain that, as long as human life continues, luck will play a prominent part in its affairs.

Disasters represent a particularly notable fork in the road of fortune because they divide those concerned into two groups: the lucky and the unlucky, the survivors and the victims. (Think here of the aristocrats of the French revolution, the kulaks of Stalin's USSR, or the passengers of a plane that crashes or a ship that founders in a storm.) When disaster strikes we face one of history's stampedes, as it were, which impels us along willy-nilly one way or the other—the way of the lucky or that of the unlucky. It is a recognition of the role of luck, more than any other single thing, that leads us to appreciate the contingency of human triumphs and disasters. "There but for some stroke of luck go I" is a humbling thought whose contemplation is salutary for us all. The trenchant question of old (posed by unfortunate and fortunate ones alike) is: Why me; what have *I* done to deserve this? The irony of course is that the appropriate and correct answer is: *Nothing*. It is simply a matter of chance—of fortuitous luck. To be sure, given our natural human commitment to the idea that we live in a rational world, we are inclined to think that there is always an ultimate reason. When things go wrong, we have a sense of guilt and burden: Why have I been selected? And when things go well, we ask: What must I now do to prove myself worthy? All of this is perfectly natural but also totally futile. The only ultimately rational attitude is to sit loose in the saddle of life and to come to terms with the idea of chance as such. Deep down we recognize full well that luck does not work by some compensating rhyme or reason. The consolation "Better luck next time" is often as not used ironically.

In a world in which we cannot help living our lives amid some degree of uncertainty, in which for any of a thousand reasons the consequences of our actions and inactions are substantially beyond our predictive reach, a reliance on luck is to some extent inevitable. Our activities can make proposals to the world, but their consequences for good or bad are almost outside the range of our knowledge and control. Be it for good or bad, what actually happens to people is all too often a matter of luck.

Like an unexpected inheritance, good luck generally comes to us unexpectedly, "out of the blue." Sometimes, to be sure, we take preliminary and preparatory steps to put ourselves in luck's way. You cannot win the lottery without obtaining a ticket or make money on the ponies without placing a bet. Sometimes you have to be in the right place at the right time. But often there is little or nothing you need to do. To have a narrow escape, for example, you simply have to avoid—by a sufficiently narrow margin—being at the wrong place at the wrong time. And, of course, an inverse story can be told with respect to bad luck.

It is often luck alone that determines the status and significance of our actions. Was that leap in the dark a stroke of genius or the beginning of the end? Was John's confession a futile gesture or a sincere act of expiation? Was Henry's decision to return to the United States in an effort to prevent Mary's hasty marriage a wise move or a step into disaster? It all depends. What descriptions fit an act will depend on the outcome, and the outcome all too often hinges on how things chance to eventuate—that is, sheer luck.

It may be chance alone—or some trivial whim—that determines whether we book the *Love Boat* or the *Titanic* for our return journey. But which way the decision goes may in fact make "all the difference in the world." In this life we are not masters of our fate—or, rather, are so only to a very limited extent. The hand of unforeseen contingency is present everywhere. The classic idea that "character is fate" is deeply problematic in all its versions,[2] because to a greater extent than any of us like to admit, it is our luck rather than our nature that determines what becomes of us in this world. Under the influence of Stoic and Epicurean philosophy, various ancient Romans saw man as a master of his fate.[3] But a different point of view was also very much astir, one according to which we are at the mercy of forces beyond our control; fate has her way with us, as she pleases.[4] "The gods knock us about like balls," said Plautus.[5] And Shakespeare tells us that we are but court jesters in the realm of Chance, ruled by a despotic monarch whose whim is our command.[6] Some of the risks we run are of our making, but most of them come our way not only unwelcomed but unbidden and uninvited, being simply unavoidable aspects of life in an uncertain and often unfriendly world.

There is no inevitable balance of luck in the natural course of things. The terrorist whose bomb explodes in the car en route to the crowded establishment where he planned to place it is unlucky. But his "tough luck" engenders many very lucky beneficiaries.

To be sure, often—in winning an heiress in competition with another suitor, for example, or in escaping unscathed from an explosion thanks to the shielding of somebody else's body—one person's good luck is attained at the cost of another's ill.[7] Jones inadvertently drops a $100 bill, and Smith finds it: lucky for the latter, unlucky for the former. But of course things need not be so—good luck can be victimless. The person who strikes oil on her own land is lucky without being so at anyone else's expense. Life is not a zero-sum game that is so arranged that the good fortune of some is necessarily secured at the expense of others. If a chance development averted an apocalyptic epidemic—or a nuclear war—everyone would be lucky, without any price being paid by particular unfortunates.

2. HOW LUCK WORKS

Luck as such is a matter of things going well or ill for someone in a situation of unexpectedness and unforeseeability. The *Oxford English Dictionary* defines the term as "the fortuitous happening of an event favorable or unfavorable to the interest of a person." Good luck is at hand whenever things go right (our desires are realized or our interests are advanced)—fortuitously, that is, in circumstances where we have no sufficient basis for confidently expecting this, because we cannot securely foresee or control the outcome. The fruits of luck (be they good or bad) are accordingly uncertain. If something that we cannot securely anticipate—let alone unilaterally control!—eventuates in our benefit, then we are lucky, and if it turns out to our disadvantage, then we are unlucky. With luck we are in a situation where the issue, to all intents and purposes, hinges on chance. For example, the would-be bank robber recognized by the newly transferred security guard who had witnessed his most recent victimization of another branch is distinctly unlucky.

While good luck is typically a matter of having things go right (or fail to go wrong) unforeseeably, "by chance," it need not necessarily be "against the odds." For sometimes people are lucky even when the odds are on their side. Samuel played Russian roulette and lived to tell the tale. He was lucky—even though only one of the six chambers of his revolver was loaded and the probabilities favored survival. For it was only "by chance" that things turned out well. Someone who escapes unharmed in a serious accident is lucky even if this occurs in circumstances where most manage to survive (i.e., where survival is likely), since it is by chance alone that our survivor is among the fortunate rather than the unfortunate. Still, when the odds are substantially favorable and the element of chance is minimal, one would more accurately call people fortunate rather than lucky. (The winner of the lottery is lucky, the loser not so much unlucky as unfortunate.)

By and large, luck is an interrupter of the usual course of things. In consequence, we are certainly not entitled to expect "strokes of luck." It is precisely because we live in a world where things do not usually turn out this way that we see good fortune as extra-ordinary and speak of "getting a lucky break." And a "streak of luck" is something even rarer and more worthy of celebration.

We are preeminently lucky whenever good things come our way unexpectedly and unprepared for—and particularly so when this happens against the odds. The golfer who manages a hole in one is the beneficiary of good luck. A lucky or unlucky event must go against the grain of rationally substantiable predictability. The winner of a lottery is lucky, but the loser who knowingly defied precipitous odds does not really qualify for a claim to bad luck—even though she is in a way unfortunate. "She should have seen it coming"—losing being so probable, was only to be expected and should have occasioned no surprise. It has been estimated that one would have to take a scheduled airline flight daily for four thousand years before an accident would occur (and even then, one has a better than even chance of survival). So we are not lucky to complete our air journey safely —though we would, of course, be distinctly unlucky to suffer a mishap.

Accordingly, luck involves the infeasibility of prediction. But an explanatory analysis of luck needs to resolve the choice among the alternatives of requiring that the lucky development be: (1) *rationally impredictable* (in a rationally cogent way by anyone), (2) in fact *unexpected* by the affected recipients, or (3) in the prevailing circumstances *rationally impredictable* by the beneficiaries—even though in principle predictable by others on their behalf. To opt for (1) here will not do, because it inappropriately rules out from being lucky the unknowing recipient whose wealthy uncle has provided right along for a big surprise benefaction on her twenty-first birthday. And (2) will not do, because it rules out from being lucky the crazy expecter who wins the lottery, having confidently (but absurdly) expected right along that this would happen. The complex combination at work in (3) provides what is, in the circumstances, the proper way to proceed.

The unexpectedness that is at issue with luck is closely bound up with ignorance. If you find yourself at a tripartite fork in the road without any idea of which of the three paths before you is the one that leads to your destination, then it is improbable (in the most objective of ways) that you will pick the right one. To be sure, the chanciness bound up with ignorance need not be an objective one (it is not really "by chance" that the roads lead where they do). But your selecting the right one is, in the circumstances, something that occurs by chance. And it is on *this* basis that you will be lucky in making the right selection. Precisely because impredictability is generally involved, people are not well advised to "trust to luck."

Deliberate effort and the exercise of skill, talent, and insight remove luck from the scene. Matters that go awry through lack of diligence, skill, and exertion—or that come right through their exercise—cannot appropriately be laid at the door of luck! The person for whom things go wrong by incompetence is unfortunate rather than unlucky, because this result is "only to be expected." But the president who has a catastrophe happen on his watch that is not of his own making—as with Herbert Hoover and the Depression, for example—is just unlucky. But there are mixed cases, too. The careless driver who has an accident in circumstances where most of the time nothing goes wrong is unlucky as well as unfortunate. Thus, even in unchancy matters, when you get things right by what is, given the inadequacy of your information, a matter of mere accident, you are still lucky.

. Attributions of luck can accordingly be defeated—or rendered inappropriate—either by showing that nothing of significance is at stake (that the outcome at issue is neither good nor bad but utterly indifferent) or by showing that the apparent impredictability at issue is not real—that in the circumstances the beneficiary involved has good reason for expecting the outcome (for example, because it is the natural result of her own efforts).

Good luck requires that the favorable outcome in view results not in the normal course of things or by planning or foresight but by "inadvertence"—by causes impenetrable to us, or, as the 1613 *Lexicon Philosophicum* of Goclenius put it, "not by the industry, insight, or sagacity of man, but by some other, altogether hidden cause."[8] Accordingly, the operation of luck hinges outcomes on what happens

27

by accident rather than by design. With luck, there must be the element of chanciness and unforeseeability, with its room for surprise. What we can reasonably expect to happen is not grist for the mill of luck. When good things are realized in the customary way through effort or bad things through mistakes, faults, and failures—that is to say, if chance is not involved—then luck is not at issue. The person who permits herself to be duped out of her life savings by a confidence man is unfortunate but not, strictly speaking, *unlucky*—as she would be if she lost it on a promising business venture (to be sure, if the con man picked her out of the crowd more or less at random, we would, on *this* basis, say that she was unlucky as well).[9]

3. LUCK VERSUS FATE AND FORTUNE

Luck is a matter of having something good or bad happen that lies outside the horizon of effective foreseeability. There is thus a significant difference between luck and fortune. You are fortunate if something good happens to or for you in the natural course of things. But you are lucky when such a benefit comes to you despite its being chancy—and particularly so if it occurs against the odds and reasonable expectations. A person who has inherited enough money to be able to travel first-class is fortunate but not lucky in the stricter sense. By contrast, the airline passenger who finds himself shifted from coach to first-class for the convenience of the airline is lucky. Fate and fortune relate to the conditions and circumstances of our lives generally, luck to the specifically chancy goods and evils that befall us.[10] Our innate skills and talents are matters of good fortune; the opportunities that chance brings our way to help us develop them are for the most part matters of luck. Contracting a cold is merely unfortunate, since it is something that people do pretty regularly, but contracting it on the evening of one's opening-night performance is distinctly unlucky.

The positive and negative things that come one's way in the world's ordinary course—including one's heritage (biological, medical, social, economic), one's abilities and talents, the circumstances of one's place and time (be they peaceful or chaotic, for example)— all these are matters of what might be characterized as fate and fortune. People are not unlucky to be born timid or ill-tempered, just unfortunate. But the positivities and negativities that come one's way by chance and unforeseen happenstance—finding a treasure trove, for example, or walking away from an accident fatal to most others —are matters of luck. It was (modestly) fortunate for John Doe that he owned a penknife. But it was distinctly lucky for him that he happened to have it along on the day he needed it to deal with a snake bite. (He didn't generally carry the knife, but just by chance took it with him on that particular day.) You are heir to a great estate by auspicious fortune, but you are lucky when you inherit it just in the nick of time to save you from bankruptcy. Luck and chance are two sides of the same coin. But fate is something else again, something from which the element of chance is missing. Suppose that we discover that a large but heretofore undetected meteor is on a collision course with the earth. Humanity's fate is sealed, the handwriting is on the wall. By a fixed number of days hence, the earth will be covered by an impenetrable cloud of debris and will become unable to sustain mammalian life. What a catastrophe! In these circumstances, however, our extinction would (strictly speaking) be unfortunate rather than unlucky. It is just the element of surprise—of chanciness and impredictability—that distinguishes luck from fate or fortune at large.[11]

The chanciness of luck means that in interactions where one party runs all the risks, only one can be lucky. The sponsors of a lottery are destined for gain—here only the players can be lucky. And the same holds for gambling casinos, where things are managed in such a way that the house "takes no chances."

And so while one can (in certain circumstances) be *fortunate* to be redheaded (say, when this makes one eligible for some benefit or other), one cannot be *lucky* to be a redhead. One can, however, be lucky in that it was redheaded individuals whom the instituter of the benefit at issue just happened to fix upon as the beneficiaries of her largesse. Luck as such must be chancy. And this is reflected in luck's volatility and inconsistency. A Scottish proverb, cited as early as 1721, says, "Behind bad luck comes good luck." (The reverse would be just as true!) And another old proverb insists, "The only sure thing about luck is that it will change."

Only if one takes too literally the idea of a *lot* in life—by (quite absurdly) thinking of human biographies in terms of a lottery of life-plan allocations to *preexistingly* identifiable individuals—can one conceptualize a person's overall fate or destiny in terms of luck. For only then would the sum total of all the goods and evils befalling people become reduced—comprehensively and automatically—to a matter of chance allocation. This is obviously unrealistic. Accordingly, a person can be fortunate to have a good disposition or a talent for mathematics, but she cannot be *lucky* in these regards, because chance is not involved. Her disposition and talents are part of what makes her the individual she is; it is not something that chance happens to bring along and superadd to a preexisting identity. One can indeed be lucky to encounter a person who induces or helps one to develop a talent. But having that talent itself is a matter of fortune rather than good luck. It makes no sense to assimilate personal fate to games of chance, because with games there is always antecedently a player to enter into participation, while with people there is no antecedent, identity-bereft individual who draws the lot at issue with a particular endowment. One has to be there to be lucky. One is, no doubt, fortunate to be born in a wealthy, technically advanced country rather than into a primitive tribe whose members eke out a meager existence. But while this is indeed fortunate, it is not really a matter of luck. It is not as though there were some world-external, fertilization-preceding version of oneself who has the luck to draw a good assignment.

To be sure, the distinction at issue is not purely and wholly a matter of reporting the actualities of usage. A slight bit of verbal legislation is involved. When we ask the girl who tells us that she has just become engaged, "And who's the lucky man?" we should, strictly speaking, say "*fortunate* man" if we wish to avoid any hint of suggestion that he picked her name out of a hat. The distinction here drawn between luck and fortune on the basis of the chanciness of the former is honored in common usage by the occasional breach.

4. WHAT IS LUCK?

"Nothing ventured, nothing gained." To "try one's luck" from time to time is perfectly sensible—though to "trust to luck" as a systematic policy is clearly foolhardy.

What is luck? In characterizing a certain development as lucky for someone, we make two pivotal claims:

- that as far as the affected person is concerned, the outcome came about "by accident." There has to be something impredictable about luck. (We would not say that it was lucky for someone that their morning post was delivered to their house—unless, say, virtually all the mail was destroyed in some catastrophe, with some item of urgent importance for them as one of a few chance survivors.)
- that the outcome at issue has a significantly evaluative status in representing a good or bad result, a benefit or loss. (If X wins the lottery, that is good luck; if Z is struck by a falling meteorite, that is bad luck; but a chance event that is indifferent—say someone's being momentarily shaded by a passing cloud—is no matter of luck, one way or the other.)

Luck accordingly involves three things: (1) a beneficiary or maleficiary,[12] (2) a development that is benign (positive) or malign (negative) from the standpoint of the interests of the affected individual, and that, moreover, (3) is fortuitous (unexpected, chancy, unforeseeable).

Luck thus always incorporates a normative element of good or bad: someone must be affected positively or negatively by an event before its realization can properly be called lucky. It is only because we have interests—because things can affect us for better or for worse—that luck enters in. A person is not ordinarily lucky to encounter pigeons in the park or to see a cloud floating overhead, since such things do not normally affect one's well-being. (It would be different if one had a bet on the matter.)

Where no one can tell whether the developments at issue are good or bad for the individuals involved—where everything is ambiguous and obscure, with no way of telling whether what happens is for better or for worse—luck is out of the picture. Take the Don Quixote of Cervantes's classic tale. With any ordinary person, those bizarre episodes—the famous encounter with the windmills, for example— would be a misfortune. But for the knight-errant of La Mancha, with his nuttiness (*locura*) and his weird way of regarding things, it was perhaps all to the good as a demonstration of the seriousness of his commitment to his knightly mission. The uncertainty that prevails here as regards the question of fortune or misfortune serves to hold the issue of luck in suspension: the prospect of benefit or loss is crucial to the operation of luck. An inert thing—a rock, say, or a hammer—cannot be lucky. To be sure, things can happen that preserve or damage it. But the absence of any element of affectivity means an absence of interests and thereby rules out the operation of luck.

Insofar as one can equate "the failure of a bad thing to happen" with "the happening of a good thing"—and consequently also equate "the failure of a good thing to happen" with "the happening of a bad thing"—these direct and indirect modes of luck will become identified. (And this seems plausible, since the just-indicated equation—failed negative = realized positive—seems wholly appropriate.) To fail to lose may not be a form of winning, but it is nevertheless a positivity of sorts. In any case, good luck resides not only in an actual gain of some sort but also in running a risk of loss and getting away with it.

Was Columbus lucky in discovering America? That he came on the continent fortuitously is beyond doubt. But the matter of evaluation is complex. It seemingly depends on the time horizon. In the short run, it lifted him to fame and fortune as "admiral of the ocean sea." In the medium run it brought him untold misery and endless troubles for the rest of his life. In the long run it gave him immortal fame. Generally speaking, however, whether an eventuation is lucky or unlucky is a matter of its immediate rather than its ulterior developments. It is unlucky for you to have a storm flood the basement of your house even if in the course of making repairs you chance to come across a treasure. The latter piece of good luck may *outweigh* the former piece of bad luck, but does not unravel its status as such.

5. LUCK AND THE EXTRA-ORDINARY

Much of human life is a matter of routine, of matters running along foreseeably in their natural course. And this is how it has to be. For without such routine—without habit and regularity and normalcy—human life as we know it would scarcely be possible. If eating bread nourished us one day and killed us the next, if our neighbor were a mild-mannered friend one moment and a homicidal maniac the next, human life and human society would not endure—indeed could not have developed in the first place. But the regularity—the normalcy —of established order does not have it all its own way in the human realm. Chance and accident frequently intrude to upset the apple cart, producing "out of nowhere," as it were, developments that profoundly affect our weal and woe. And it is just here that luck comes upon the stage. For luck and fortune are notoriously futile. As Horace put it: "Fortune, happy in her cruel work, and obstinate in playing her perverse game, ever varies her unsteady honors, favoring now me, now someone else."[13]

34

Luck is the antithesis of reasonable expectation. It manifests itself most strikingly with situations that are predictively counterindicated—eventuations that are surprising by virtue of their flying in the face of plausible forecasts. Some prime examples of events that ought to surprise us are those that are beyond our control and those whose eventuation is inherently *chancy*. Luck thrives in the gap between probability and actuality, between what can reasonably be expected (what "ought by rights to happen") and what actually occurs. When these two agree, then luck is out of it. (As we have seen, the individual who has a foreseeable gain is thereby fortunate, but not lucky.) But when goods and evils befall us in circumstances where actuality is out of tune with reasonable expectation, then luck, be it good or bad, is upon the scene.

However, a happy or unhappy development can be a matter of luck from the recipient's point of view even if its eventuation is the result of a deliberate contrivance by others. (Your secret benefactor's sending you that big check represents a stroke of good luck for *you* even if it is something that *he* has been planning for years.) Thus even if someone else—different from the person affected—is able to predict that unexpected development, the eventuation at issue may still be lucky for those who are involved.

The factor of impredictability is crucial for luck in providing for the essential contrast with "what is only to be expected" for good and sufficient reasons. There are two major sources from such lack of predictability: chance and ignorance. As to the first, it lies in the nature of the case that when something happens by genuine stochastic chance, it cannot confidently be predicted once the odds are sufficiently low. (Of course, when a chance development occurs with 99.9 percent probability, we can safely predict it with high, albeit not absolute, confidence.) The second main route to unpredictability is ignorance, for this too restricts the range of what can securely be predicted. When you confront a fork in the road and cannot tell which way leads to your destination, then even though there is no chanciness about where the roads lead, it will be purely "by chance" that you pick the right one. So we need one single word to encompass both chance-impredictability and ignorance-impredictability, and the term *fortuitously* will serve the purpose. When you pick the right color at roulette (where success depends on chance) or the right fork in the road (where success depends on guesswork), we may say in both cases that your getting it right was fortuitous. And either way, that fortuitously successful issue was a matter of luck.

There are, in general, three routes to realizing the good things of life such as health, wealth, success, and the like: in theory we can achieve them by effort and hard work (the old-fashioned way!), by coming into them through good fortune (by accident of birth and inheritance), or by obtaining them through sheer luck—by winning in the "lottery of life." Usually—for most of us and for most of the time—good things are realized only by the expenditure of effort and through planning, toil, and persistence. Luck represents a way of getting there more easily—through a "gift of the gods," as it were. (And, of course, it works both ways; what good luck gives, bad luck can take away.) Luck thus affords us what is, in a way, a shortcut to the achievement of life's good things. With good luck we get something for nothing—an unexpected and undeserved boon. Normally, good things come our way through our abilities and efforts, and bad things befall us in consequence of our faults. But luck provides an alternate route. For one who has its favor, "a pocketful of luck is as good as a sackful of wisdom" (as the proverb has it). When one correctly rec-

36

ognizes one's good luck, the natural reaction is not only one of surprise but also one of pleasure. To have a boon bestowed on one as a sport of circumstance—unbidden and unanticipated—is something one is bound to find pleasant.

Among American presidents, Ulysses S. Grant was fortunate because the war plucked him from obscurity and positioned him for the office, but Harry S. Truman was lucky in arriving there through a series of accidents, which put him in the vice presidency at the time of Franklin D. Roosevelt's death. Since luck involves matters eventuating for better or worse in unforeseeable ways, it transpires that people have to be accounted lucky when they succeed in life beyond the level of reasonable expectation that their inherited endowments and acquired condition would indicate. And those who fail beyond the level of reasonable expectation that their faults, shortcomings, and personal deficits would indicate have to be accounted unlucky. Insofar as things run in the way that is normal, natural, and only to be expected, luck is not present on the scene. Luck involves departures from the expectable, and its place on the stage of human affairs is assured by the fact that the conditions of life are erratic— be they social or political or meteorological, things simply do not always run in their usual and regular course. Even Homer occasionally nods, and even a Muhammad Ali or a Pete Sampras can have a day off from his usual unbeatable form.

Whatever good luck provides us with is a free gift; to the extent that luck is indeed involved, it requires no investment of talent or effort, and no merit is at issue. And whatever bad luck deprives us of also leaves our merits untouched; no diminution of desert or worth is at stake. Luck affects our personal condition but does not reflect our personal worth. Abraham Lincoln, James Garfield, and William

McKinley were killed by assassins' bullets. Theodore Roosevelt, Harry Truman, and Ronald Reagan survived assassination attempts (in Truman's case, he was wholly untouched—here, too, he was lucky). In this context, no particular merit attaches to the one side of this dichotomy and no special fault to the other. When we say that that was how the luck of the matter chanced out, we have said it all.

Chance is most strikingly manifested when improbable circumstances are actually realized. We are particularly lucky when things turn out well despite our inaction or—even more so—despite our ill-advised and misguided actions. And we are particularly unlucky when things turn out ill despite our doing all the right things. The sick person who recovers swiftly despite taking the wrong medicine is very lucky; the one whose ailment worsens despite all the proper medications and treatments is distinctly unlucky. In such cases, the commonsense logic of the situation points one way while the decrees of fate point another. The workings of luck are clearly manifest in those good and bad developments, which ought, "by rights," not to be there at all.

Among a thousand stocks some are pretty well bound to go up and others down—even in the best and worst of times. Every share of every one of these stocks is bound to be owned by *somebody*. So there will always be winners and losers. And, given the unforeseeability of the matter, the difference between them will generally depend on luck alone. The fund managers who happen to hold winners obviously like to claim a special talent or insight. But that seems farfetched in the circumstances (at any rate, insofar as efficient market theory has it right). Only someone who is able to turn in a superior performance for over a sufficiently long, virtually chance-excluding period of time would be in a position to stake a really plausible claim to success on the basis of skill rather than luck.

A background of normalcy and reasonable expectation is crucial for luck. The person who manages to walk away from an airplane crash is lucky in having this narrow escape. But the person who safely completes such a journey is not thereby lucky—having achieved no more than what is normal, natural, and expected. Again, someone who searches for a needle in a haystack and finds it straightaway is lucky, seeing that this goes counter to what we would expect in the circumstances, namely having to spend a long time hunting about. And the person who has to spend forever at it—who does not find that needle until the final straw of hay is turned over—is thereby unlucky. Good and bad luck are defined against the background of normal expectation and generally run against its current.

How we fare in life—what our future will be—depends not on our nature alone (on what we *are*) but also on circumstance—on those chancy opportunities that may or may not allow us to bring our nature to its natural expression. Our condition on the world's stage is the product of *fate* (what we are), of *fortune* (the conditions and circumstances in which we are placed), and of *luck* (what chances to happen to us).

Luck thrives on vulnerability, and people are more vulnerable in some times and conditions than in others. One salient question for luck is accordingly whether we live in *normal* or in *extraordinary* times and circumstances—in "quiet" times or in times of war, revolution, and Sturm und Drang, which by their volatile nature create a greater scope for luck. Only when things go normally and take their ordinary course will our "nature" be able to predominate here. In extraordinary times and under extraordinary circumstances, the volatility of conditions will destabilize the usual course of things. The rogue factors chance and luck now come to the fore. The extent to which there is room for luck in life is itself at the disposition of fortune. The circumstances of life that set the stage for fortune and luck alike are by no means a level playing field. (The imprecation "May the natural consequence of your folly befall you!" is one thing, while that of the Chinese proverb "May you live in interesting times!" is something quite different.)

II

F A I L U R E S   O F   F O R E S I G H T

1. THE LIMITS OF PREDICTABILITY

L uck—unlike good or bad fortune—is annihilated as such by fore-sight. If I know that I will win the lottery tomorrow (because I have been able to "fix" it), then I am perhaps fortunate but not lucky. If I am to be hung tomorrow for being a horse thief, then I am obviously unfortunate but not unlucky. Luck has to come on its recipient's unawareness. The positive and negative developments one can (appropriately) foresee are not matters of luck.[1] But whenever foresight fails us in matters that bear on our weal or woe, then we are under luck's sway. In consequence, luck's presence is pervasive in human affairs because our predictive capabilities are decidedly lim-ited.

To rely on luck alone is clearly to court disaster, seeing that im-predictability here lies at the heart of the matter. For better or for worse, we live in circumstances where obstacles to successful predic-tion reside both in the nature of things and in our own cognitive limitations. Natural impediments to prediction obtain insofar as the future is *developmentally open*—causally undetermined or underde-termined by the existing realities of the present and open to the contingencies of chance or choice. Cognitive impediments obtain insofar as the future is *epistemically inaccessible* to us, which may occur because we do not know the operative laws (uncertainty) or the requisite data (pre*dict*ive myopia), or else because the inferences and calculations needed to obtain answers from laws and data involve

41

complexities beyond the reach of our predictive capabilities (incapacity). Either way, rational prediction becomes infeasible. And on this basis those notorious prediction-spoilers of ignorance and contingency (chance, choice, chaos) create scope for luck. It is instructive to consider somewhat more closely these principal obstacles to achieving effective insight into the future.

2. ONTOLOGICAL IMPREDICTABILITY: CHANCE

Chance opens the door to luck. When the chances are against success and it nevertheless occurs, you are lucky. Conversely, if the chances favor success and nevertheless it fails to ensue, you are unlucky.

Chance is clearly one of the prime factors that limit our capacity for prediction. It is a matter of unruliness in the phenomena themselves; its operation roots in the objective, ontological makeup of things. The processes of a world pervaded by chance and chaos—not to speak of the vagaries of human agents—are in substantial measure genuinely *random* (or *stochastic*) in not conforming to any sort of definite, outcome-determinative rule. Where predictability is not just impracticable but actually infeasible, the world can, in theory, proceed from a fixed past to distinct but altogether feasible futures: one selfsame history can, in principle, have different continuations. Insofar as developments root in this sort of random causality, they thereby preclude any prospect of firm rational prediction. (Though of course we may be able to estimate probabilities.)

In a related but decidedly weaker sense, some developments are characterized as matters of "chance" not because they fall outside the lawfully regular cause-and-effect framework of events, but because they depart from the way in which affairs *normally* and *ordi-*

narily proceed in the domain of phenomena at issue, so that the usual bets are off. (A good example in human affairs would be the assassination of a key political figure.) Strict chance means that the actual laws of nature fail to be future-determinative; this presently envisioned weaker mode of chance means only that the usual and familiar regularities fail to be so. (It is generally only in this weaker sense that a chance encounter between people is chancy.)

Chance does not preclude correct prediction. Will a six come up when you toss the die? By responding yes or no randomly, you will often get it right. Occasionally you may also have a spectacular string of successes. It's just that you won't get it right "more often than by chance." And that is exactly what rational prediction is about—getting things right more often than would be accounted for by chance. Where chance is at work, secure prediction thus becomes infeasible. No one can predict tomorrow's stock prices in a reliable manner. Even the fullest knowledge of contemporary medicine provides no secure means for forecasting the future course of human diseases in particular individuals. And even the best-informed student of public affairs cannot predict with confidence what tomorrow's headline will be.

Determinists exile chance altogether from the world's scheme of things because they hold that the shape of the future is preordained: world history is preprogrammed from the very outset—be it through necessitarian scientific law (as with Pierre-Simon de Laplace), or the ordinances of a controlling deity, or through the inexorable decrees of fate, destiny, or "the stars" (as with traditional astrology). The die is cast; our future is already settled—and there is nothing further to be done about it. What is to be is and ever has been unalterably predetermined to be, and that's that. On such a view, people are not

43

masters of their fate and shapers of the eventuations that transpire on the world's stage; the most we can manage is to do willingly whatever it is that has been preordained: like it or not, things must go on their inevitable way, and we along with them.[2] We can align our thoughts with the world's course of events, but we cannot alter it. This in effect was the doctrine of ancient Stoicism, and the position of Spinoza in the seventeenth century was not far removed from it.

A *deterministic* world then is one where chance plays no part—one that is (in principle) *completely* predictable, so that there is no room for surprise for a sufficiently powerful intellect with a comprehensive knowledge of the past. Such a world opens up the prospect of dispensing with probabilistic considerations because predictive issues can in theory always be settled decisively one way or another. But to whatever extent a world falls short of this idealized state—as this world of ours to all appearances substantially does—impredictability will come upon the scene, and luck is bound to appear in its wake.

The fact is that recent physics has come to see our world as indeterministic. It emphasizes the role of chance and stochastic randomness in the world's eventuations, stressing those numerous physical phenomena which, like quantum processes, are inherently probabilistic. We should not (for example) ask for a prediction of the time when a certain atom of an unstable transuranic element will disintegrate into simpler components, because such a time cannot in principle be predetermined. From the perspective of contemporary physics, the prominence of stochastic processes in nature force us to turn from exact forecasts to probability distributions. Even before the rise of quantum theory, the accepted gas laws were already statistical. And the same was already true of the entropy law in thermodynamics and Josiah Willard Gibbs's phase rule in chemistry. Step-by-step, modern science has been moving away from determinism and toward a doctrine of chance limited by law. And, of course, the operation of chance is not confined to physics alone. In biology we see randomness at work in genetic mutations; in economics there is the random-walk theory of stock-market price fluctuation; and so on. Chance is a pervasive factor in modern science—witness the diffusion of probabilistic and statistical techniques throughout this domain. To be sure, different ranges of phenomena vary sharply in the scope that they provide for chance: it is obviously greater in politics than in celestial mechanics.

However, while individual chance events are indeed unpredictable, the very randomness of chance fluctuation means that large-scale phenomenology may well be predictable via the "laws of chance" codified in probability theory. Chance obviously *can* block the path to prediction, but it certainly need not necessarily do so. In quantum theory—for example—it is eminently unlikely that an atom with a half-life of a week will still be around a year later. We therefore could—and would—confidently predict that it will not be. What is lacking here is not predictability but rather fail-proof certainty on the one hand and definiteness of outcome on the other. Chance and indeterminacy open the gate to impredictability, though perhaps not quite as wide as one might think at first, seeing that chancy (i.e., probabilistic) predictions can often be made with reasonable assurance. But, of course, impredictability of any manner or description opens a doorway to the entry of luck.

Chance has a way of making shambles of our best-laid plans. For this reason, reformers and idealists never feel comfortable with its existence and would like to exclude it from their ideological constructions. Utopians—and perfectionists of all sorts—have little use for luck.

Genuinely chance-dependent outcomes are not controlled or determined by anyone—not even by God. But, as sagacious theologians have long noted, this does not mean that the operation of divine providence is excluded in a situation of chance. For one thing, it could well be owing to a divine decree that a certain development is left open to chance. And even when God does not *determine* a chance outcome, he might nevertheless be able to foresee its eventuation, because foreknowledge as such is not necessarily causative. It lies in the nature of things that *we* cannot predict chance outcomes correctly more often than chance itself indicates. But there is, in theory, no reason why this disability need hold for God.

3. CHAOS

Chaos too paves the way for luck by presenting a major impediment to prediction. A physical system is said to be *chaotic* when its processes are so highly sensitive to conditions that very minute differences in an initial state can nevertheless engender very great differences in result, with minuscule local variations amplifying into substantial, large-scale differences in eventual outcomes.[3] The flow pattern of cigarette smoke, or the motion of a blown-up toy balloon released with an open end, are typical examples. Here even the most exact achievable measurement of initial conditions would not be sufficiently precise to make it possible to predict the patterns of motion.

Modern physics accordingly inclines to see nature as a terrain that contains widespread pockets of predictable stability within a larger environment of unpredictable chaos—a realm in which the possibilities of prediction are thus decidedly limited in scope. The weather is a good example of a chaotic system, where small changes in an initial state can engender great differences in the result. And this sort of situation is pervasive in human affairs. Very small differences in how we act or react to what occurs about us can make an enormous difference in the result. The slightest misstep can lead one to catch his heel, trip up, and break a leg. Small fluctuations can have big consequences: the slightest change in timing could make the difference between meeting and missing the person who might be one's spouse. The impredictability of chaos (in this somewhat technical sense) pervades our human affairs and provides yet another reason why luck is destined to play a major role in our lives.

Chaos is by no means an uncommon situation in nature—witness the flashing of lightning, the falling of leaves, the shifting of cards, or the diffusion of plague. In many social processes we encounter factors so minute as to seem negligible, which can nevertheless become amplified to the point of making an enormous difference in the course of events. To be sure, chaos must be distinguished from indeterminism. A process is indeterministic if *one and the same (literally identical) set of initial conditions* (i.e., one selfsame circumstantial state of affairs) can eventuate in different results. By contrast, a process is chaotic if minutely different, *observationally indistinguishable initial conditions* can eventuate in different results, irrespective of how sophisticatedly we make the observations (short of unrealizable idealizations). The timing of heavy-element disintegrations is an example of the former situation; the swirling of cigarette smoke one of the latter. Such chaos is prominent not only in nature but in human affairs as well. It occurs not just on our roads and highways but in human interactions at every level.

Even where the linking equations are completely deterministic (and so, even in a Laplacean world of classical physics), prediction will nevertheless be infeasible with chaotic systems because of the physical impossibility of effecting perfectly precise measurements.[4] In particular, this means that no model that one could ever make of a chaotic process (whose condition would, after all, always at some point differ from that of the system in some small way) could ever be used as an instrument for reliable prediction. The weather is a good example of chaos. As one exposition puts it:

> Why have the meteorologists such difficulty in predicting the weather? Why do the rains, the storms themselves seem to us to come by chance, so that many persons find it quite ridiculous to pray for an eclipse? We see that great perturbations generally happen in regions where the atmosphere is in unstable equilibrium. The meteorologists are aware that this equilibrium is unstable, that a cyclone is arising somewhere; but where they cannot tell; one-tenth of a degree more or less at any point, and the cyclone bursts here and not there, and spreads its ravages over countries which it would have spared. This we could have foreseen if we had known that tenth of a degree, but the observations were neither sufficiently close nor sufficiently precise, and for this reason all seems due to the agency of chance.[5]

In such chaotic systems, even a minute variation in one's assessment of a system's initial state can make for a complete blur in one's predictive vision of future conditions.

In nature we often encounter what mathematicians call *exponential instability*, arising where a certain quantity can fluctuate over a sizable range every fixed period: say, where each day the region of uncertainty manages to double. After two days the quantity can be anywhere in a region of radius 4, after three days of radius 8, etc. So after a month the region of uncertainty has a radius of roughly 3,300 million. With phenomena of this sort, the tiniest fluctuation can, in theory, engender a cataclysm. A small twinge can cause a person to misstep and slip into the way of an onrushing car. A small gust of wind can make the difference between a bullet's hitting and missing. In such matters, our forecasts are inevitably probabilistic. Traffic accidents and victimization through criminality are prime examples here. And since the complexity of the phenomenon means that we cannot measure with precision exactly how much consumer credit prevails in the economy of today, we cannot forecast the result of policies that ease restrictions on credit yet further, since these will often depend in a very delicate way on currently available credit. Chaos (in this somewhat technical sense) pervades our human situation and means that luck—that is, the impetus of *chance* on matters of human weal and woe—seems to play a major role in our lives.

Often chaos masquerades as chance. Even in a causally (or, for that matter, theologically) deterministic world, many eventuations can appropriately be regarded as happening "by chance" *from our human point of view.* For their embedding in that world's causal (or rational) structure will lie above and beyond the reach of any observations and discriminations that we ourselves could possibly manage to make. Such eventuations—albeit in themselves *determined*—are bound to figure in our thinking as matters of fortuitous chance, because (by hypothesis) their *determining* is beyond our powers, so that no amount of planning or foresight on our part can play any effective role in the matter. In the end, then, chaos is no less serious an obstacle to prediction than outright randomness, with the result of providing yet another reason for the prominence of luck in human affairs.

4. CHOICE

In general, systems whose development is self-determined—whose modus operandi evolves over time in ways proceeding spontaneously from within an otherwise inscrutable interiority (and thus in a manner significantly independent of the external circumstances under which the system operates)—will for this very reason function in ways that are not completely predictable for external observers. Human choice is one particularly striking example of this phenomenon. For insofar as your intentions are opaque to me, I cannot reliably forecast your actions.

To be genuinely human is to be an autonomous free agent. This, of course, does not necessarily mean being unpredictable. Indeed, our foresight into our own intentional future actions, and even those of other people, is often better than our foresight into many other things, and there is thus ample scope for predicting human behavior.[6] If I know your taste in books or in films, then I can confidently predict your free selections among alternatives—and will probably be right much of the time. We can safely predict of a sensible person that she will freely choose to do those things which are—in the circumstances—the sensible things to do. Moreover, there is no phenomenological (observational) difference between a regularity engen-

50

dered by a preprogrammed mechanism and one that is produced by a free agent who has decided upon following some rule. But all the same, free will does open up room for defeating predictions. Once I realize that a predictor claims that I shall do X, I can deliberately defeat this forecast by refraining from doing so—even though this may well be an art of mere cussedness that means that I shall have to cut off my own nose to spite her.

But what of the specter of fatalism? Perhaps all of our choices are somehow preprogrammed by the world's causal processes? What price free will then? The first point is that insofar as choices and preferences figure among the causes at issue, there is no problem for free will. It is only the prior determination by extra-volitional (agent-detached) causes that would create a difficulty. But more important yet, even here—even if (as Spinoza has it) our choices were constrained by *ex ante* causality—freedom of the sort relevant to matters of responsibility and morality would not be abrogated. For this sort of freedom actually demands not *exemption* from causality as such but only the availability of a workable contrast between *agent-detached* causality (owing to factors like compulsion, posthypnotic suggestion, and the like) and an *agent-involving* causality geared to wants and wishes. A free act—in the relevant sense—is simply one that is *not* done, owing to causes detached from the agent herself in one or another of a spectrum of specifiable ways. In consequence, it could not have been predicted for certain "on general principles" without detailed information about that particular agent—information of a sort that, in general, we can obtain only with great difficulty, if at all.

What their free will generally enables people to do is not so much to choose unpredictably in the ordinary range of cases but to choose impredictably in some extra-ordinary ones. Jean Buridan's famous example is doubtless right—an ass may conceivably starve between two equally appealing bales of hay. But a human free agent will certainly not do so. Or again, in suitable circumstances we may "choose" to put our free will into suspension and hand the selection over to an impredictable random device—say a coin toss. It is less the operation of our free will than the prospect of our willful and deliberate suspension of its operations that can render human actions unpredictable.[7] (I can freely delegate my choice in various interactions to the outcome of a coin toss.[8]) Yet even here, it is the agent herself with whom responsibility for the working out of her own destiny lies.

To be sure, even where individual agents behave in erratic and unpredictable ways, this need not preclude predictability in the aggregate. For as long as those eccentricities cancel out at the collective level so as to become lost in a statistical fog, we can obtain perfectly stable large-scale effects. We cannot forecast individual suicides or robberies, but we can certainly predict the statistical rates. The impredictability of free agents in some aspect of their individual comportment is perfectly compatible with the predictability of large-scale, aggregate effects. Still, all in all, there is no question that the free actions of agents can be volatile and that actual results can fly in the face of plausible prediction.

And so people's capacity for free, predictively intractable choice also comes to function as yet another of the major sources of luck. For in any situation where the results of one's own actions depend on the impredictable actions of others, one has no alternative but to deem oneself lucky when matters eventuate to one's own satisfaction (and unlucky in the reverse cases). When it launched the Edsel automobile in the wake of market studies indicating public demand for yet another low-priced behemoth gas guzzler, the Ford Motor Company was not careless but just unlucky.

5. IGNORANCE

With chance, chaos, and choice all conjointly at work, we live in a world that is inherently unamenable to prediction and that thereby creates room for luck. But no less crucial in this regard is the sheer human ignorance that inheres in our pervasive lack of information —the fact that Homo sapiens is also *Homo ignorans* means the inability of agents to foresee (and, all the more, to control) the course of events in which their interests are engaged. Ignorance—the lack of information—is yet another prime obstacle to prediction.

Perhaps Einstein was right in insisting that God does not play dice with the world. But this makes little difference to luck. For us, ignorance has the same effect as chance. Even in a wholly deterministic world, we are still lucky when we chance to guess right by accident alone. And when our best-calculated and most prudently managed risks go wrong, we are still unlucky. If one does not know the laws at work, one cannot predict the resultant phenomena. And even if one does know the laws and general principles at work, one may be unable to predict just when the conditions to which they apply will be realized. If I don't know what you want to say, I cannot begin to predict the words you will use. Either way—be it from lack of understanding of the operative laws or from lack of information about the prevailing conditions—ignorance proves a decisive impediment to secure prediction and thereby constitutes yet another prime basis for luck.

Unbeknownst to you, your rich Uncle Arthur has for years been planning to give you a surprise gift of one thousand dollars on your twenty-first birthday. When the time arrives, it is certainly a lucky day for you—who had no reason to expect this development—even though it happened by a long-laid plan known to various relations. Luck here roots in the lack of advance information on the beneficiary's part rather than in outright unforeseeability in the abstract. Again, you want to go to Cincinnati (never mind why!). You go to the station in complete ignorance of the railway schedule and get there just in time to catch the only train for the day, thus realizing your aim by dumb luck. Of course, had you *known* that this was the right time for the train, then luck wouldn't have come into it. But as it was, the matter was otherwise.

Luck is not a force, factor, or agency of some sort. We would be ill advised to reify—let alone personify—it. It is simply a reflection of a fact of life. All those innumerable obstacles of prediction—ignorance, chance, choice, chaos, etc.—mean that there is bound to be much that is crucially important for us that we nevertheless cannot manage to anticipate. Many of our actions—perhaps most of them—are to some extent stabs in the dark, akin to shooting at a target we cannot see clearly. And hitting the bull's-eye in such circumstances is exactly the sort of thing that luck is all about.

It cannot be overemphasized how deeply luck roots in sheer ignorance. Luck takes over where knowledge, foreseeability, and reason no longer furnish us with secure guidance. And given the incompleteness and imperfection of our knowledge, such limitations are unavoidable. And so, while people have always sought to minimize impredictability's scope through recourse to oracles, astrologers, spiritualistic counselors, expert advisers, and the like, the fact remains that our predictive incapacities have to be recognized as an ineliminable fact of human life. Our cognitive and practical impotence vis-à-vis the future is simply a bitter pill we have to swallow.[9]

This line of thought makes it clear that insofar as luck roots in *eliminable* ignorance, the attainment of knowledge can put it out of operation. But our prospects here are unfortunately limited, since so much of our ignorance regarding the world's ways is simply ineliminable in the circumstances in which we actually find ourselves. In this world, much of what happens in matters that affect our needs and wants will, in significant measure, lie outside the range of our knowledge and control. We humans are beings with limited capacities to obtain, process, and exploit information. The prospect that things will eventuate to our advantage or disadvantage in ways we do not anticipate is pervasively ever-present. And as long as surprising occurrences can impinge upon us in matters that affect our interests positively or negatively, we remain at the mercy of luck. Luck is therefore something that roots deep and secure in the condition of Homo sapiens.

This is particularly manifest in the context of complex social systems where many individual agents interact, each with its own idiosyncratic aims and purposes, and each with its own personal body of information and misinformation. I am in a tight electoral contest. You are one of the voters. But you keep your own counsel: I have no idea how you will vote, whether for me or for my opponent. I am in total ignorance on the matter—as far as I can see and tell it's fifty-fifty. But you, of course, are decided. For you, the actual voter, there is nothing chancy about it: your mind is made up. Question: If you vote for me, am I lucky? In the circumstances, the answer is clearly yes. To be sure, the outcome is a foregone conclusion so far as you are concerned; from your angle (and from the world's), there is no chance about it. But my lack of information renders it entirely fortuitous as far as I am concerned. From where I stand, the matter is altogether chancy. Luck is a matter not only of the world's arrangements but also of people's cognitive relationship to them. And their outlook thus comes into it, too. If it is your policy to trust people, then you are lucky if you encounter a truth teller in a world of liars; but if distrust is your policy, the matter stands otherwise.

Luck is bound to be present in situations of personal interaction with others, where the contingent contributions of these other agents is substantially unforeseeable for oneself. Suppose that Jim is contemplating proposing to Janet without having any confident expectation as to how she feels about marrying him. He really doesn't have a clue as to what Janet will actually do; the whole issue is an enigma for him. In these circumstances he will have no reasonable anticipation of success or failure—one way or the other. The fundamental uncertainty of the situation makes the occurrence of a positive or negative outcome a matter of good or bad luck, one way or the other.

Where the course of natural events runs on its usual, accustomed track, luck is out of the picture. Suppose an unstoppable deadly virus spreads across the planet. Our days are numbered; by some weeks hence the earth will cease to sustain human life. Strictly speaking, however, it is in terms of humanity's being unfortunate rather than being unlucky that we will have to describe this situation. Nothing fortuitous has transpired here.

One must distinguish between randomness, chaos, and anarchy. Anarchy means the total absence of law and order. Chance and chaos, by contrast, are actually orders of a sort, albeit orders of a certain (highly irregular) sort. A random sequence of 0's and 1's (say

010011101 . . .) can be purely stochastic (i.e., random), but it is certainly not chaotic. It is (by hypothesis) a linear sequence, one that consists only of integers (and indeed only two of them) rather than also having names of cities, and so on. As best we can tell, the world we live in, replete with chance and chaos, is not anarchic. However, the factor of ignorance remains, and from our standpoint it matters not whether *there are no laws* or whether we are simply *ignorant of them*. Either way, the impredictability engendered by anarchy can also emerge from ignorance. Indeed, as far as prediction is concerned, chance, chaos, anarchy, and ignorance all lead in exactly the same direction: all of them put us into a position where the rational fore-casting of outcomes is simply infeasible.

An intriguing question now arises: Does it make any difference for luck just *why* it is that the beneficiary is ignorant of that benign eventuation? Consider the following two possibilities with respect to the example of the person who missed her train because of an un-announced schedule change:

- She didn't bother to call the station. Everybody else knew about the change of schedule, but she just didn't trouble to find out. The new timing was publicized, preprogrammed, known to all con-cerned, and readily knowable for our protagonist as well. Her ig-norance of the matter was, as it were, self-imposed.

- It was a special train put on secretly by management, unannounced and unknown to the public at large. There was simply no predict-able way in which our protagonist could have found out about it.

The fact is that she was lucky either way. For luck, it makes no difference whether the eventuation was *impredictable* by nature for the agent in the circumstances or merely *unpredicted* by her. As long as the individual's success (or failure) ensues in the absence of fore-knowledge, she is lucky (or unlucky). You are lucky (or unlucky) if good (or bad) things come your way in circumstances that involve the element of surprise, relative to your information about the matter. Whenever there is actual ignorance—whatever the reason—a successful outcome will be chancy and its eventuation fortuitous. If you do not know how many people are in the next room, the correctness of your guess is a matter of sheer happenstance.

What place is there for luck in a setting where "nothing is left to chance"? Suppose for the sake of discussion that the world is the product of the operations of a benevolent, all-knowing, and all-powerful creator—or, if you prefer, of an all-determining necessity. The question now arises: What room would this situation leave for luck in the scheme of things?

To be sure, God is exempt from the operation of luck: luck is something that has no place in the affairs of an omniscient being who *knows* all outcomes, or of an omnipotent being who *controls* all outcomes. One may (in a way) be fortunate to be such a being: luck as such has no place in its life. Luck inheres in incapacity: in its absence there is no place for luck. However, the matter takes on a very different aspect from the human angle.

Even in a deterministic world, where everything is preordained in the grand programming of things, we can, nevertheless, appropriately characterize in terms of luck those benefits and negativities that come people's way wholly outside the range of their knowledge and control. Ontological determinism notwithstanding, such unexpected gains and losses would figure in our thinking as being matters of luck for *us*, because (by hypothesis) we are unable to foresee various future eventuations. It is the lack of foreseeability that is the crucial factor for luck, irrespective of whether it is objectively rooted in chance or subjectively rooted in imperfect information. Luck inheres as prominently in cognitive as in physical limitations.

The salient point is simply this—that even in a world in which everything is preplanned and somehow prearranged, there nevertheless is ample scope for luck with respect to the imperfect agents that populate such a world—agents for whom ignorance creates every bit as much room for luck as would be achieved by pure chance. And this brings us to the crucial connection between luck and finitude.

The inability to foreknow (and thereby, of course, to control) an issue in whose outcome one has an interest is crucial for luck. This disability may be either one of practice (ignorance, lack of information) or one of principle (genuine impredictability). For reasons of sheer ignorance, one cannot predict how many people will decide to sell stocks tomorrow. For reasons of principle ("chaos"), one cannot predict which horse will win tomorrow's race. Either way, if I put my money to risk and win, it will be a matter of sheer luck. The specific route to that predictive incapacity is immaterial. The outcomes are fortuitous either way. You play roulette, betting on red. The wheel is fixed and—unbeknownst to you!—red is predestined. When that ball comes to red, there you are, lucky nonetheless. For you did not know—and, in the hypothetical circumstances at issue, could not have known—that this was going to happen. The definitive conditions of luck are all operative: seeing that what we have here is (by hypothesis) a favorable outcome that the affected individual was unable to foresee. To be sure, it was your guess of red—and not the wheel's coming up on the color—that was the lucky event.

6 . HOW IMPREDICTABILITY DIFFUSES

Our ability to foresee developments runs into problems whenever the issue depends sensitively on assessing causal factors which themselves depend on other equally sensitive factors. Thus, consider: Will the world's food supply be adequate in the year 3000? Resolving this predictive issue in a sensible way calls for assessing a whole host of parameters: *population* (reproduction rates, emergence of new diseases, wars), *agricultural production* (climate, soil-conservation practices), *availability of animal foods* (sea and land organisms), *conditions of life* (quality of life [crime, pollution], economic conditions [employment]). Now it is evident that each of these items will itself depend on further complicated (and sometimes imponderable) factors: each will itself hinge on further estimates which themselves involve substantial elements of unpredictability. Overall, our predictive prospect here very much depends on climate changes, chemical and atomic warfare, the impact of meteorites, and a thousand and one other factors which themselves are difficult, if not impossible, to foresee. (And matters get even worse, since there are cyclical feedback interconnections with any such systemic issue.) The predictive problem with which we began crumbles between our fingers into a vast proliferation of others.

Consider another example of such an explosion of predictive parameters. To forecast the demand for consumer durables, one has to take into account the general condition of the economy with special reference to consumer credit and employment, as well as demographics, technological innovation, changes in fashion, and myriad other factors. And each of the factors in turn will itself hinge on other complicated—and often predictively recalcitrant—factors. We thought we had one predictive problem on our hands but now find that it has exfoliated into a number of others, each of which exfoliates into various others, each of which has its own problems and difficulties and many of which belong to domains very remote from that of the first. In such cases, we find it somewhere between difficult and impossible to get the predictive process satisfactorily under way. Issues of this parameter-cascading sort can prove to be totally beyond our predictive reach because they confront us with a pileup of errors, as one imperfect estimate repeatedly compounds with yet another.

This brings us to an ominous fact. Once present for *any* reason—chance, choice, uncertainty, or whatever—impredictability always ramifies over a far wider domain. For the world's processes constitute a fabric of cause-and-effect interconnections within which all those impredictable occurrences themselves proliferate further causal consequences that are thereby also bound to be impredictable. And this circumstance vastly amplifies the impredictability at issue with chance, choice, and their congeners. It means that once impredictability gains *any* foothold at all, it can ramify, spreading like wildfire to diffuse itself throughout the environing domain of cause-and-effect relationships.

For reasons of this sort, the prospect of predictive inadequacy surrounds us on all sides. And so when our policies in individual or social action (be it in personal investment or in national economic policy) turn out "according to plan" in such matters of predictive complexity, we have every reason to congratulate ourselves for being lucky.

7 . MISPREDICTION: PREDICTION SPOILERS

Luck calls for the absence of foreseeability. It deserves to be stressed that all these various obstacles to prediction can also function in a very different way—not just as *impediments* to rational prediction but as *spoilers* that lead otherwise perfectly good and appropriate predictions to go wrong, causing our responsibly made predictions to meet with unexpected disaster. For example, we predict (perfectly reasonably) that Frank will be here soon—after all, we saw him in the distance coming along the road. But he is suddenly felled by a car gone out of control. Here chance aborts an altogether appropriate prediction. Again, we predict (perfectly reasonably) that Peter will pay off the small sum he owes us—after all, he has done so on numerous past occasions. But this time it just so happens that temptation gets the better of him and he chooses to use the money to buy another stamp for his collection. Here choice aborts a perfectly sensible prediction. Then, too, ignorance (and its cousin misinformation) can also operate as a prediction spoiler. Believing in astrology, we predict a victory on the battlefield—but that, alas, is just not how things work in the world, and our prediction goes awry.

The long and short of it is that all the factors that constitute obstacles to the prospect of prediction can also operate at a different level to produce mispredictions by invalidating people's inherently sound and sensible expectations. The prospect of successful prediction is not just at the mercy of human frailties by way of bias and wishful thinking, but even more decisively at the mercy of the human limitations inherent in our emplacement in circumstances that make prediction generally difficult and often impossible *in principle,* thereby creating openings for the sorts of surprises that lie at the very heart of luck.

It might seem that the obstacles to successful prediction are so numerous in variety and so extensive in scope that here, as with Dr. Johnson's dancing dog, it could be said that what is surprising is not that it should be done well but that it should be done at all. As Rousseau wisely observed, "The ability to foresee that some things cannot be foreseen is a very necessary capacity." Still, evolutionary considerations will also have to be kept in mind. Our human predictive capacity may be severely limited, but it is not—and in the circumstances cannot be—altogether nil. If we humans were not as good at prediction as we are, and did not live in an environment that makes predictions possible in substantial degree, then we would not be here to tell the tale as the sorts of intelligence-guided creatures we are. It is utterly implausible to think that creatures whose actions are guided by beliefs could make their way successfully in a complex and often hostile environment by luck alone.

Be it for good or bad, luck is a fact of life whenever predictability fails us. And the limits of predictability are set both by objective and by subjective factors—they reside both in the nature of the world and in the nature of the would-be predictors who function within it. On the objective side we have the three C's of contingency: chance, chaos, and choice. On the subjective side we have the factors at issue in our cognitive imperfections, in particular, ignorance, error, bias, and misinformation. That things work out for the good or ill of beings operating in these conditions is bound to be a matter of hit or miss. Both of these sorts of limitations accordingly engender the impredictability that is pivotal for luck.

Matters of chance and luck have often been endowed with predictive power. Games of chance—with dice, pebble casting, or cards—all originated from efforts to obtain predictive omens: they were used as informative (future-indicative) resources before becoming mere pastime amusements. But of course this pairing of luck with fate is mere superstition. Insofar as genuine chance is at work in matters of luck, this cannot possibly furnish insight into the futurity of human affairs. Chance is never more than that—mere chance—and cannot as such speak with the voice of destiny.

It lies in the conceptual nature of things that matters of luck are predictively intractable. There are circumstances in which one can appropriately say to oneself, "If I do A, then I *may* be lucky"—say, in the context of putting money on a racehorse. But there are no circumstances in which one can appropriately say to oneself, "If I do A, then I *will* be lucky." If a secure prediction could be made about the matter, then it would not be appropriate to characterize it in terms of luck.

8. LUCK AND HUMAN FINITUDE

Attributions of good or bad luck can be defeated in many different ways. But the pathways to defeat are readily classified. For an outcome to involve luck, two things are required: (1) that it be *significant*—that we have a stake in it in that it makes a difference, that it matters to us one way or the other, and (2) that it be *fortuitous* and involve the element of unforeseeability, unpredictability, or chance. Attributions of luck can accordingly be defeated on either count. The outcome may make no difference (as when it matters not where that falling leaf settles to the ground). Or the outcome, though of material importance for us, may be predictable through being something that was only to be expected, either because it results from the exercise of conscious control (by way of the deployment of effort, skill, planning, and the like) or because other factors (personal or natural) have been operative to produce it in ways that we could and should have anticipated.

Suppose someone says: "We are going to play a game that involves your transforming a number according to certain rules. You pick the number—any one you like. And then if you get the original number back after the transformation, I'll give you one hundred dollars." Now consider this arrangement to be implemented by the following family of instructions:

1. Pick a number (*any* number).
2. Multiply it by itself.
3. Add 1 to the result of step 2.
4. Divide the result by two.

Suppose that you now (at step 4) get your original number back. Was this result obtained by luck or by chance? Clearly by chance alone. It would not and could not possibly have happened if the number you had picked had not been 1.[10] Chance is the determinative factor here.

By contrast, consider the following family of instructions:

1. Pick a number (*any* number).
2. Multiply it by itself.
3. Add 1 to the original number.
4. Multiply the result (of step 3) by itself.
5. Subtract the result of step 2 from the result of step 4.

65

6. Subtract 1 from the result (of step 5).
7. Divide the result by two.

Again, suppose that the result is the original number once more. This time, however, the upshot is the product not of chance but of necessity. It would have happened *irrespective* of the particular number you initially picked.[11] Chance has nothing to do with it here.

In the second case, then, luck is apparently out of the picture. But here appearances are just a bit deceitful. For in cases of ignorance luck steps upon the scene once more. If you play the game in the second manner, you are lucky even here precisely because you had no idea what sort of process would be at issue when you initially entered into the game. As far as you are concerned, it is a matter of mere chance that the situation happens to be of the second type rather than the first. Someone who bets that a red card will be drawn from a card deck is lucky even if (unbeknownst to them) all the black cards have been removed. For while the outcome is inevitable and as such devoid of chance, our bettor's having chosen the right way relative to that deck-modification occurred (so we will suppose) by pure chance. Luck requires the element of impredictability—but this can obtain even in situations where the particular outcome may not be chancy in and of itself when chance enters in through the back door of ignorance.

To be sure, the world being what it is, the factors that could set luck aside are frequently absent. Our lives are lived in a world whose eventuations often fall outside the range of our productive power or predictive foresight—a world whose complex and capricious modus operandi puts the future beyond our grasp. Our aims and goals, our "best-laid plans," and indeed our very lives are at the mercy of accident and unmanageable contingency. In such a world, where the outcomes of all too many of our actions depend on "circumstances beyond our control," luck is destined to play a leading role in the human drama—collective and individual alike.

Luck pivots on incapacity—on the existence of human limits. If we knew what was going to happen, either through predictive power or through effective control over our own destiny, there would be no place for luck. For luck turns on the pervasive prospect that fateful things can happen without our expecting them. In the final analysis it is this lack of information rather than the three C's of contingency that is crucial for luck. The aim of science, Hegel tells us, is to reduce the scope of chance.[12] But there is only so far we can go.[13]

One of the most fundamental features of the human condition is exactly this circumstance of our finitude—the fact that we are limited creatures who have a decidedly limited cognitive and practical control over our fate and our future—creatures at the mercy of developments largely outside the sphere not only of control but also of knowledge and even reasonable expectation.

Two sorts of disabilities impede our being "in control" of our lives: limitations of knowledge and limitations of power. (They are closely interrelated: power is useless without knowledge, and knowledge itself is a mode of power.) Now insofar as we are not in control (either operationally or cognitively), we cannot foresee outcomes. And insofar as this transpires—insofar as the outcomes of our actions are hit-or-miss in relation to our intentions—successful action will fall into the sphere of luck. The ultimate reason why luck cannot be exiled from the sphere of human concerns lies in the imperfection —and, given the role of chance and chaos in nature, imperfectability—of our predictive foresight. What we cannot foresee we cannot control, and where we cannot establish control we must to some extent depend on luck to yield favorable results.

Hope and apprehension are therefore bound to play a significant role in our lives. We play our own cards as best we can, but the outcome will depend on what is done by the other players in the system—be they people's actions or nature's developments. In innumerable ways we are impotent, unable to control the things that befall us on the world's stage. The proposing may be ours, but the disposing lies with nature, circumstance, and the actions of others— all unfolding in ways over which we expect little, if any, power. Luck accordingly represents one of the salient factors that characterize the human condition. Whenever unforeseeable and thus also uncontrollable developments affect us for weal or woe, we are through this very fact caught up in the web that luck spreads throughout the realm of human affairs.

III

THE DIFFERENT FACES OF LUCK

1. MODES OF LUCK

"Lucky at play, unlucky in love," says the proverb.[1] Luck operates in many different contexts; there are almost endlessly varied ways of being lucky or unlucky. But the vast majority of them fall into a comparatively small number of identifiable types.

To begin with, it is necessary to distinguish between luck proper and luck in a broader sense that also includes fate and fortune. Fate is a matter of natural, innate advantages and disadvantages (for example, being born as the heir to a great estate; having innate skills and talents of various sorts). The endowment with which one is born—specifically, one's talents, abilities, and capacities—is a matter of fate, be it kindly or otherwise. Fortune is a matter of acquired advantages or disadvantages, be it due to effort or to external circumstance (for example, being present at the place and time of a natural disaster). The circumstances and conditions that enable one to bring one's capacities to fruitful realization—or that operate so as to frustrate this endeavor—are matters of fortune. Fate and fortune define the world's plan for us, so to speak; they determine who we are and the circumstances in which we live.

Fate and fortune all too obviously treat us unequally. Some people are emplaced in a locale that becomes a war zone, while others occupy a habitat pervaded by blissful peace and quiet. And even as some of us are positioned in the wrong place, so others are emplaced in the wrong time. Unkind fate or uncooperative fortune may have it that another Marlborough or Napoléon languishes in obscurity in time of peace. The question pivots on personal assets and circumstantial opportunities.

But luck proper is something else again. Its domain begins where fate and fortune leave off. It relates to the fortuitous goods and bads that mere accident brings our way, irrespective of the impetus of personal effort and encountered stage setting. For luck turns on life's exceptions and relates to the things that chance to happen to us within the context defined by fate and fortune. Fate and fortune determine the rules of the game for us; luck engenders the exceptions.

Luck comes in many different forms. The most important and distinctive ones form a rather long list. It includes: *windfalls and wind thefts* (for example, stumbling upon a treasure; having one's house destroyed in a plane crash), unforeseeably *lost and gained opportunities* (for example, failing to recognize a good investment opportunity; coming down with a disease for which a cure has just been discovered), *accidents* (for example, catching one's heel in a crack and taking a bad fall; getting caught up in an automobile chain collision), *narrow escapes and flukish victimizations* (for example, selling one's securities on impulse just before a crash; being the victim of a random act of violence; coming down with the flu on the day of the award ceremony), *coincidences*—just happening to be at the right/ wrong place at the right/wrong time (for example, getting elected president on the eve of a depression; eating at a restaurant on the evening the soup went wrong; getting struck by lightning—in a location where one would not ordinarily expect to be vulnerable), *consequence-laden mistakes in identification or classification* (for example, being wounded by an assassin who mistakes one for someone else; or being the mistaken recipient of a benefit due another), *fortuitous encounters*, be they happy or unhappy—chance meetings with agents or agencies that make an impact upon one's life (for example, having a singing telegram delivered by the person who becomes the love of one's life; arriving at the check-in counter just at the moment when the airline needs to transfer a passenger to first-class), *welcome and unwelcome anomalies*—exceptions to general rules and the usual course of things (for example, having one's lost wallet returned unpilfered; being imprudent and getting away with it, or, "getting away with murder"; ignoring the rules with impunity). Luck accordingly involves quite an extensive taxonomy, which deserves a closer look.

A windfall—an unexpected inheritance, for example—is a particularly striking form of good luck. Suddenly, a significant benefit comes one's way unexpected and unbidden, like a gift from the gods. Surprised by the surprisingly enthusiastic reception of *Childe Harold*, Byron declared: "I awoke one morning and found myself famous." Such unanticipated revolutions of circumstance typify what good luck is all about. However, there are not only windfalls but also "wind thefts," which manifest the less happy prospect of a penalty imposed by unforeseen developments—the loss in the mail of one's insurance renewal on the eve of a fire, for example. After all, whatever good luck may give us, bad luck can (unfortunately) manage to take away.

Unforeseeable opportunities for gain and loss represent yet another major form of luck. Someone who happens, quite by chance, to acquire a commodity for which fortuitous circumstances create a seller's market can be considered very lucky. On the other side, the householder whose neighbor's son decided to take up the drums just as she was putting her place on the market was distinctly unlucky.

71

Accidents are one of the most common and familiar forms of bad luck. They occur in an almost endless variety of ways. Some are trivial—cutting oneself shaving, say, or having soup spilled on one's necktie when a careless waiter bumps one's elbow. But others can prove fatal. In the United States, we lose hundreds of workers to industrial accidents each year and more than three hundred people to traffic fatalities each holiday weekend. Unless they "asked for it," as people sometimes do—for instance, by driving long highway stretches alone when very tired—these accident victims were simply unlucky. The system demands, as it were, a certain number of sacrifices, and they came out on the wrong side of the lottery of death. But while we cannot control accidents—more or less by definition —we nevertheless certainly can often control the *risk* of accidents. (If you drive only half as far, you run only half the chance of an automotive mishap.) People are sometimes accident-prone to the point of being accidents waiting to happen because of inattention, carelessness, and incompetence. The probabilistic chances of mishap are so loaded against such individuals that when things go wrong one might more accurately characterize them as unfortunate rather than unlucky. Be that as it may, the fact remains that we live in a world where all too often things go awry despite our most plausible expectations, because, as the proverb has it, "There is many a slip 'twixt the cup and the lip."

A narrow escape is a mishap that almost occurred but happily did not. A person is lucky in this manner when saved from misfortune by some fortuitous event—a chance occurrence, a haphazard eventuation, somebody's unexpected mistake, or the like. The visitor who by chance left the area just before an earthquake struck or the potential victim saved because a would-be assassin missed the bus are cases in point. Such lucky escapes are commonplace, but some are more dramatic than others. Colonel Frederick D. Grant, oldest son of the United States president, served as an aide to General George A. Custer, commander of the Seventh Cavalry. However, he happened to be absent when this unit was annihilated by Chief Crazy Horse and his Sioux Indians in an ambush at a ravine near the Little Bighorn River in Montana. A day or two before the Seventh Cavalry set out on its attack, Grant received "compassionate leave" to be at the bedside of his wife, who was about to give birth to their first child. By pure chance, Grant's eagerness to play the good husband saved his life.[2]

Those who have a narrow escape are lucky, but those who have a wide escape—who simply were never at risk in the first place—are merely fortunate. You were inadvertently delayed and just missed crossing on the *Hindenburg,* so you were lucky. But if you were the sort of homebody into whose mind the very idea of a transatlantic voyage never entered, you were (in this particular regard) merely fortunate.

The inverse of a narrow escape might be called a "flukish victimization." An example would be the person whose car stalls when crossing the railway track just ahead of the arrival of the 12:16 express. Or the youngster who just has to sneeze at the moment when the big line of the school play must be delivered. Developments of this sort are one of the most painful forms of bad luck—and frequently have disastrous consequences. (Falling victim to the haphazard impact of a tornado is a particularly striking example.[3])

Coincidence—being at the right or wrong place at the right or wrong time—is a particularly notable form of luck. Captain E. J. Smith, who on the verge of retirement signed on for his career-crowning command on the maiden voyage of the "unsinkable" *Titanic,* was distinctly unlucky, and so was the person who just happened to be passing underneath the parapet when an icicle dropped off. And the author whose biography of a celebrity hits the bookshops just as its protagonist is enmeshed in a highly publicized scandal is lucky and can laugh all the way to the bank. With luck, as the saying has it, "timing is everything."

Cases of mistaken identity are yet another important source of good and bad luck. The person who inadvertently receives the boon that is intended for another (think of Isaac and Esau) is eminently lucky. The fighter pilot whose chance encounter with turbulence leads him to hit the eject button instead of the defroster is unlucky. (Presumably, much care goes into the design of equipment to minimize the prospect of such mishaps.)

Fortuitous encounters represent so striking a class of luck-engendering coincidences that they deserve a special category. Chancing to drop in at a party affords one person the opportunity to meet his spouse-to-be and affords another the chance to make a contact that leads to a profitable business deal. Good luck for them! By contrast, the burglar who breaks into a house just before its owner returns well-armed from a bear hunt is distinctly unlucky. A graphic example of a fortuitously fortunate encounter is cited by a nineteenth-century moralist:

A village apothecary chanced to visit the state apartments at the Pavilion [in Brighton], when [King] George the Fourth was seized with a fit. He bled him, brought him back to consciousness, and by his genial and quaint humor, made the king laugh.

The monarch took a fancy to him, made him his physician, and thereby made his fortune.[4]

The writer goes on to observe, "Predictably no man ever lives to middle age to whom two or three such opportunities do but present themselves." This may be a bit overoptimistic, but the fact remains that fortuitous encounters represent one of the principal ways in which luck impacts on our lives, for good and bad alike.

Often luck pivots on anomalies. The person who (like Rasputin) somehow manages to survive a deadly dose of poison is an example. The luck at issue here is determined as such against a background of normal expectations. (Large doses of strychnine usually kill people off.) Such lucky anomalies (or exceptions) are a matter of being spared by a generous fate from the adverse consequences of actions or omissions of a sort that usually issue in misfortune. The girl who marries a man who drinks too much but successfully gives up alcohol in order to please her is very lucky, since she manages to come out on the right side of very long odds. So is the foolish lad who pays someone twenty dollars for a share in the Brooklyn Bridge and, when he goes to claim it, finds a fifty-dollar bill on the walkway. And so is the careless individual who leaves his wallet behind on the bus but has it returned in the mail a few days later with its contents intact. Lucky anomalies of this general sort are a close cousin to narrow escapes.

When we go against the rules—of prudence, logic, strategy, or whatever—and *things nevertheless work out all right*, we generally have good reason to consider ourselves lucky. Breaking the rules and getting away with it is one of the prominent and pervasive forms of luck in human life, but either way, being exempted from the natural consequences of one's action—be they for the good or for the bad —betokens the entry of luck upon the scene. (To be sure, with situations of anarchy—where the rules exist in name only and are "made to be broken"—there is no room for luck by way of violating rules and getting away with it.)

There are also, of course, unlucky anomalies, when things chance to go wrong against all ordinary expectation—as with the passengers of a hijacked airplane. Acts that have unintended and unforeseeable unhappy consequences often fall into this category. Thus, if Tom insults Bob intentionally (to pay him back for an earlier insult) but finds that (despite thinking him thick-skinned) Bob reacts so violently that he dies of a stroke, we have to deem both Tom and Bob unlucky on grounds of the significant anomaly at issue. And, inversely, the person who takes every responsible and sensible precaution and nevertheless sees things go wrong is extremely unlucky.

The reality of the situation is that the lucky individual often fares better with modest talent than the unlucky one manages to do with fortune's gift of greater abilities. Opportunities taken at the tide lead on to success. And the person who fails to capitalize on the possibilities that happen to arise—who squanders the gifts of chance— has much to lament.

The relationship of luck to control is complicated. Causal responsibility for an eventuation in itself does not necessarily remove luck: if it was by sheer accident that you pushed the button that averted disaster, you were still lucky. Nor does intention of itself remove luck. If you intended to divert the runaway train from a crowded intersection by pulling a certain handle and succeeded, you might still have been totally lucky—if, for example, the switch you pulled was the wrong one, but your pulling it by some fluke stimulated somebody else into pulling the right one. For control to take luck out of the picture when an action realizes a significant outcome, this control must be exercised not only effectively but appropriately as well.

So much, then, for luck's principal ways and means. The significant fact is that a relatively small number of categories can evidently accommodate the vast majority of instances in which good and bad luck are at work.

2. REAL VERSUS APPARENT LUCK

It is unforeseeability *from the standpoint of the recipient*—the beneficiary or maleficiary—that is standardly at issue with luck. The unlucky victims of a planned and managed catastrophe—the farmers starved by Stalin or the victims of Hiroshima—are caught up in a disaster that is not in itself fortuitous or unpredictable. Those who arranged for the catastrophe at issue were amply informed in advance of what was to happen, seeing that they planned it. But those who were affected were caught unaware, and in calling them unlucky we adopt their point of view.

Yet suppose something happens that significantly affects someone and is foreseen and expected by this person, while nevertheless the expectation is wholly inappropriate and unwarranted, as with someone who "knew right along" that he was going to win the lottery and "was completely certain of it" from the very start. Is this (badly deluded) individual actually lucky or not? The answer becomes clearer on closer inspection. Take our strange friend Robinson. He thinks that someone who both sees a rainbow and finds a four-leaf clover on the same morning is bound to succeed with whatever he undertakes that day. So on the day he experiences such a happy conjuncture, Robinson buys a lottery ticket—and he happens to win. Of course, he is not at all surprised. Matters here eventuate exactly as he thought: winning is entirely in line with his confident and unhesitating expectation. As he sees it, luck has nothing to do with it; he felt sure of winning from the outset. But, of course, we know better. An important lesson is at stake here—that of objective versus subjective luck, of *actually* being lucky as against merely *thinking* oneself so. To be authentically lucky, the benefit must be real and the impredictability must be reasonable. The person who mistakenly believes herself poisoned and then mistakenly believes that some unexpectedly acquired substance provides the antidote needed to save her life undoubtedly *thinks* herself lucky but in fact is not actually so. True luck is a matter not of expectation alone but of *reasonable* expectation.

Luck, as we have seen, involves the chancy occurrence of something harmful or beneficial. And as regards both chanciness and eventuation there can be biases and errors of assessment. The fact is that both probabilities (likelihoods) and utilities (positivities and negativities) can be assessed either objectively, as they actually are, or subjectively, as someone thinks them to be (perhaps mistakenly). One must accordingly distinguish two situations:

objective luck: both probabilities and utilities are assessed objectively

subjective luck: either the probabilities or the utilities are assessed subjectively

To be realistic (in one of the key senses of this equivocal expression) is to close the gap between the subjective and the objective: to bring one's personal expectations and estimations into line with the actual objective realities of the case. With genuine luck, this involves getting both the utilities and the probabilities right.

Consider the following situation. Bernard thinks of the sun as a fire. And he thinks that, once extinguished, it will never light again. Now comes a total solar eclipse. The sun's light is extinguished. But lo and behold, a minute or two later it returns—wholly contrary to Bernard's expectation. He thinks there has been a flukish flare-up, so that he is very lucky—and the rest of us with him. Yet clearly it is not so.

Or consider Juliana. She overhears some ignoramus tipster who claims it is a sure thing that Lightning Jack will win the fourth race. She takes this as gospel, adjudges this nag's victory a sure thing, and proceeds to bet the family farm. And Lightning Jack wins. Juliana deems herself fortunate all right, but nowise lucky. (What's lucky about the success of a sure thing?) But she is simply deluded.

Again, consider Julian, who gets the evaluations of a situation wrong rather than its likelihoods wrong. He very much wants something that is, in fact, bad for him and very much against his interests (e.g., to have more booze to drink; to marry Jane, who is "all wrong for him"). Unexpectedly, Julian manages to secure this "benefit" and realize his wishes. Is he lucky? He will certainly *think* himself lucky. But there is evidently a difference between real and merely apparent luck, between actually *being* lucky and merely *thinking* oneself to be so—a difference that reflects the distinction between real and apparent benefits. What counts for real (as opposed to apparent) luck is the impact on the actual (objective) *condition* of the beneficiary rather than what he happens (subjectively) to think about it. (The alcoholic who wins a free pass to the happy hour at the local bar is not particularly lucky.)

What counts for (real) luck is—clearly—a realistic appraisal of the predictabilities involved. With luck, as with so much else in life, there is accordingly a significant difference between the real and the apparent. One can *think* oneself lucky without actually *being* so—witness the person who "finds" money she put in her purse yesterday and forgot about. And, of course, one can be lucky without recognizing it. All this is simply a consequence of the distinction between objective and subjective luck—of how things actually stand for an individual and how they may *seem* to this person.

Luck is a state of affairs and not a state of mind. One can be lucky and not realize it; one can *think* oneself lucky and not actually be so. Here, as elsewhere, the subjective view of things need not coincide with the objective facts.[5]

3. CATEGORICAL VERSUS CONDITIONAL LUCK

The matter of benefit and harm that is crucial to luck is less straightforward than it seems. Some developments are positive or negative in themselves—gaining one thousand dollars, for example, or getting a shot. But some are only positive or negative in a certain context, given that something else also happens: they are good or bad "in the circumstances" or "considering the alternatives." If one had every expectation of gaining ten thousand dollars, then gaining one thousand dollars is a distinct disappointment. If one has been poisoned, then getting the injection of an antidote would be a distinctly welcome development.

This duality of fortune carries over to luck. It would not ordinarily be a piece of luck to be "nearly frozen to death being tossed in a small lifeboat for several hours on a stormy night in the Atlantic." But to the person for whom this experience is a means to rescue, such a development would or could well be a piece of good luck.

One is *unconditionally* lucky (or unlucky) when something intrinsically good (or bad) happens fortuitously. Finding a treasure trove is a piece of unconditional good luck; stumbling and breaking one's arm a piece of unconditional bad luck. By contrast, one is *conditionally* lucky (or unlucky) if that fortuitous bit of good or bad fortune is good or bad only on the basis of some extraneous considerations. Good luck can occur within bad luck or bad luck within good. Steve was involved in a major train wreck but by a fluke escaped unhurt. Jane won the raffle and received an all-expenses-paid vacation in a tropical paradise, but she was bruised when caught up in a political demonstration there. Missing the bus is bad as such, but would be a good thing if the bus later plunged over a precipice. Winning the girl is all well and good, but might be a bad thing if it leads to one's being stabbed to death by a jealous rival. Collateral circumstances can radically alter the luck status of particular developments.

In any realistic appraisal of the luck situation, the relevant contexts of conditionality have to be taken into account. Consider the following sequence of developments:

A. You decide to travel to Dobney, near Boston.
B. You choose to travel to Boston on the 3:15 train.
C. Your cab breaks down en route to the station and you miss the 3:15 train.
D. You wind up having to take the next train, at 4:45.

E. The 4:45 runs into a two-hour delay en route.
F. The 3:15 train was wrecked and many passengers injured.
G. To make up for lost time, you take a cab from the train station instead of proceeding by bus.
H. Your cab has a flat that takes an hour to repair.

Quite an adventure, that! Note that the following circumstances obtain:

1. Certain of these eventuations were unconditionally unlucky for you, namely, C and H.
2. Certain of these eventuations were conditionally unlucky for you given others, namely, B given F, F given B, D given E, E given D, G given H, and also A given B and F.
3. Certain of these eventuations were conditionally lucky for you given others, namely, C given F.
4. None of these eventuations were unconditionally lucky for you.
5. Some of these eventuations were unconditionally unlucky for some people, namely, F (though not for you, because you were not involved).
6. None of these eventuations were unconditionally lucky for anybody.

You certainly had some hard luck here. Almost all the developments at issue were somehow unlucky for you—F is the sole exception, since you were not immediately involved! (And F is certainly an unfortunate development in and of itself.) From your point of view, virtually everything that happened was unlucky. But, nevertheless, there is one piece of good luck for you, conditional though it be— C given F—which atones for all the rest. Despite the long series of mishaps and misfortunes, you had the good luck of a narrow escape from disaster. This one piece of good luck clearly outweighs all the rest and serves to make you lucky overall. In a complex transaction of this sort, it is ultimately the size of the biggest piece of luck involved that determines the subject's overall condition of lucky versus unlucky.

With luck, it is the strongest link in a chain of circumstances that proves determinative. Thus, if someone in a disaster comes out well contrary to any reasonable expectation, he is in fact lucky—though, of course, this is not because of the disaster but because of that unexpected sequence of events that turns a minus into a plus. And similarly with the reverse situation. Finding that golden nugget is not really all that lucky for Tex if he manages to get killed by robbers on his way to the assayer's office.

Luck is something that does not hinge on individual outcomes in isolation: its attribution is unavoidably context-dependent. For one thing, whether or not some apparently lucky development is indeed a good thing may well depend on the time horizon, with one sort of resolution indicated in the short run and another in the long. What looks like a benefit or loss can actually turn out to be otherwise. The country that wins a battle in its war with a bitter enemy may deem itself fortunate in the short run but may well have to think otherwise in the long run if this victory simply prolongs the agony of a sure and increasingly costly defeat. It was, in fact, fortunate for Germany that its major offensives in the east (Moscow) and the west (the Battle of the Bulge) were unsuccessful. For had the war's end been delayed—even merely by a matter of months—the atom bombs that descended on Japan would almost certainly have devastated Germany. And as with fortune, so with luck. It too involves a comparable complexity. Think of the person who wins the jackpot but falls victim to a disgruntled gambler sworn to kill the next big winner. There is little one can say here except that he was lucky to win (how can we say otherwise?) but extremely unfortunate to do so at a time when that crazed lunatic was at large. Likewise, the winner of a lottery who uses the proceeds to fund a dream retirement cottage on Krakatoa finds the fruits of her luck turning to ashes.

Good luck can easily turn sour. One has the impression that only rarely do people react to windfalls by way of constructive life-style changes.[6] There seems to be no systematic study of, for example, lottery winners. But anecdotes abound. The brother of one winner of the Pennsylvania lottery hired a hit man to murder the winner and his wife. And many lottery winners spend a good deal of time in court fending off ridiculous claims (including one from a lottery winner's friend who had been asked to pray for success).[7] A sequel of bad luck does not unravel an initial success as the item of good luck it indeed was—even as a hollow victory, it is still a victory of sorts —but it does cause the positivity at issue to unravel. A piece of good luck is not always what it seems. In context it may prove a disaster. The proverb has it right: "You never know your luck 'til the wheel stops."[8]

4. THE MEASUREMENT OF LUCK: FORTUNE AND PROBABILITY AS LUCK-DETERMINATIVE FACTORS

Luck obviously comes in very different shapes and sizes. On the currency exchanges, one person gains and another loses a million dollars. The child whom one courageous swimmer saves may be that of a pauper who gives thanks, while the child saved by another may be that of a magnate who gives a princely reward. In the ordinary course of things, we have no hesitation about treating luck in quantitative terms speaking unhesitatingly about a little or a lot of luck coming someone's way. When we are hunting for a word in the dictionary and chance to open the book to the right page, we are lucky all right, but in a rather small way. Can this idea of measuring luck be implemented with some degree of clarity and precision?

The two crucial factors that determine the operation of luck are: (1) making a significant difference for weal and woe, and (2) going against the perceived odds, against what can reasonably be anticipated from the beneficiary's perspective. The first and crucial issue obviously relates to the size of the benefit or loss at issue. But probability enters into the picture as well. For someone is lucky or unlucky to the extent that something good or bad—something fortunate or unfortunate—comes his way despite its being improbable. And, in general, the less the likelihood of an outcome that is to a fixed extent beneficial (or negative), the greater is the good (or bad) luck at issue in its realization. It is thus evident that two principal factors are operative in the idea of luck: (1) *fortune* (good or bad), and (2) *probability* (or, rather, improbability). In determining the magnitude of luck, these two factors must both be weighed on the scale. Even when a benefit is small, we will still be lucky when it comes our way against great odds. And when a potential loss is very large, we will still be lucky to avert it even if the probability stands in our favor. (The person who survives an operation whose fatality rate is only one in a thousand is still *somewhat* lucky.)

It is apparent on this basis that an eventuation which makes a great positive difference for a person's fortunes *and* is unlikely is a very lucky one for this beneficiary, and that one which makes a great negative difference *and* is unlikely is a very unlucky one. Thus, consider the youth whose proposal of marriage has been accepted by the girl of his dreams. He deems himself "the luckiest man in the world" precisely because he saw this eventuation as highly unlikely, since he could not really persuade himself to believe that so splendid a creature would accept someone as unworthy and undeserving as he. Again, the trader at Barings P.L.C. who in early 1995 bought many hundreds of millions of dollars of financial derivatives tied to the Japanese economy was eminently unlucky. For the stakes were huge and the probability very small for a mishap on the scale of the earthquake that devastated Kobe and roiled the Japanese financial markets.[9] We are, it is clear, particularly lucky (or unlucky) when we sustain a very substantial gain (or loss) in a manner that goes decidedly against the apparent odds. And it is part of our human reality that this can and does happen.

IV

AN INFINITY OF ACCIDENTS

1. THE PROMINENCE OF LUCK IN HUMAN AFFAIRS

Just exactly how prominent is luck in human affairs? Admitting that an element of unmanageable unforeseeability pervades all human affairs, Renaissance humanists often inclined to the optimistic view that rational endeavor can prevail against the slings and arrows of outrageous fortune. For example, Poggio Bracciolini (1380–1459), in his tracts *De miseria humanae conditionis* and *De varietate fortunae*, championed the efficacy of rational virtue: "The strength of fortune is never so great that it will not be overcome by men who are steadfast and resolute."[1] Fortune as such is no more than the product of the interaction between human reason and nature's forces—both products of God's endowment of his world. Others took a much less sanguine line. Thus in Chapter 25 of *The Prince* (1513), Machiavelli, after surveying the cruelties and haphazards of the politics of his day, set more pessimistic limits to human endeavor by assigning half of what happens in this domain to the intractable power of *Fortuna*, with her rogue force partially tamed by prudently installed dikes and embankments.

It is, of course, next to impossible to specify the relative proportion of what happens to people through fate and fortune, through actual effort, and through simple luck. Ironically, the luck-effort ratio itself seems to be at the mercy of fortune. There is no stable ratio to fix the relative contribution of luck and labor in life by determining how large a part of what becomes of us is due to our efforts (or lack thereof) and how much is due to mere chance. For this proportion is variable and alters with the shifting sands of conditions and circumstances. In "ordinary" times and situations, ability and effort will be predominant; when the course of relevant events is "normal"—when things by and large go "according to plan"—the role of luck is minimized, though certainly not annihilated. Times are in fact "normal" exactly to the extent that they allow people to realize their potential—to get what is fitting with respect to their merits and demerits rather than be deflected from their proper condition by good or bad luck. On the other hand, in volatile times—periods of revolution, war, riot, and disaster (natural or man-made)—what becomes of people will generally be a matter of mere chance. When catastrophes occur, it may well be mere accident that distinguishes between survivors and victims. Here luck predominates. There is, to all appearances, little that can be said about the matter at the level of unqualified generality.

This being so, there is ample room for a luck-desert debate running parallel to (and not wholly disconnected from) the nature-nurture debate. For luck is, clearly, yet another factor opposed to both nature and nurture that plays a decisive role in determining a person's career in this world. And the respective prominence of luck versus labor in life is itself one of the characteristic features of the circumstances of place and time. *The scope for luck in life is itself at the mercy of fate and fortune.* In times of war, plague, or natural disaster, effort counts for little, and luck is everything. In times of peace, prosperity, and normalcy, the scope for luck is reduced, and skill and effort come to play a larger role. We are fortunate indeed if we live in circumstances where we are ourselves masters of our fate and need place only minimal reliance on the aid of luck to have things work out to our satisfaction. People who have good luck are indeed fortunate, but those who have only a modest need for it are perhaps even more so, seeing that they are only minimally at the mercy of mere chance. Only in normal conditions and benign circumstances do people have the opportunity to "show what they are made of."

It does seem, however, that modernity's scientific and technological progress has significantly affected the scope of luck in human affairs. Consider the milestones of life: birth, coming of age, training and career choice, marriage and children, aging, final illness, and death. Some element of chance is operative at every stage. But in settled, advanced societies today, success in matters like reaching adulthood and finding employment suited to one's interests and talents is nowadays more probable. This clearly differs from the situation of the past—and from the situation in underdeveloped countries. In this regard, then, the onset of modernity has changed the impact of luck on the condition of people living in advanced countries by providing a more user-friendly environment for people. (To be sure, there is the other side of the coin, represented by modernity's unleashing of the ever more powerful destructive forces available for warfare, terrorism, and technological disasters.) Still, it is a matter of degree. There is no getting around the fact that much of what happens to us in life—much of what we do or fail to achieve or become—is a matter not of inexorable necessity or of deliberate contrivance, but one of luck, accident, or fortune.

2. LUCK IN SETTINGS OF COMPETITION AND CONFLICT

It is worthwhile to consider at least briefly the ways and means of luck in some of the special areas of human endeavor. For luck takes many forms and is able to adjust its coloration, chameleonlike, to the background of various settings.

Luck in Games. Success or failure in situations of competition and conflict often hinges on matters of fortuitous happenstance. Even in conflicts of skill rather than chance—especially in sport and game competitions—luck plays an enormous role. A player's momentary distraction here or accidental slipup there can open up the opportunity for his opponent to add a decisive point to the score. When the opposing team's star player happens to have an off day, our team may win the point that gains the championship. Games between evenly matched teams, where victory is not a foregone conclusion owing to an imbalance of skill, are interesting precisely because the role of chance eventuations—and thus of luck—is so prominent. And it is an easy step from sport to the more serious conflicts at issue with—

Luck in Warfare. There is enormous scope for luck in warfare. An accidentally intercepted message may betray plans and intentions to the enemy; a tactical maneuver gone wrong through a fluke may create a decisive opportunity for the opponent in battle. The fog of unknowing that covers the battlefield opens doors beyond number for the entry of luck. And in war, timing is everything. It was a piece of very bad luck indeed for General Robert E. Lee at Gettysburg that General J.E.B. Stuart decided to take his cavalry off raiding instead

90

of providing scouting cover for the invading Confederate army. It was a piece of very good luck indeed for the Americans at Yorktown that the British under General Cornwallis made their foray before the French fleet under Admiral de Grasse had to return to its winter station.

A mode of warfare somewhat different from the military is the political. Here, too, there is ample scope for luck, as, for example, with—

Luck in Elections. The democratic electoral process obviously affords enormous scope for the operation of luck. A candidate's ill-timed flu can reopen large questions about her state of health. Bad weather on election day may favor a liberal candidate by keeping the more conservative elderly voters at home. In the 1890–1930 era, Democratic candidates did not have much of a chance in U.S. presidential elections. One of the cardinal reasons why "a week is a long time in politics" (as the saying goes) is that fortuitous developments here have the prospect of widening the road for luck.

Luck in Search and Research. Be it in prospecting or in scientific investigations, many search processes have a hit-or-miss aspect that allows substantial room for the operation of luck. Scientific discoveries are often made not on the basis of some well-contrived plan of investigation but through some stroke of sheer luck—a phenomenon common enough that a specific term has sprung up for it, and such discoveries are said to be made "by serendipity."[2] This occurs in science when investigators come upon answers to questions or solutions to problems by sheer haphazard rather than by design, planning, contrivance, and the use of methods. Consider such dramatic examples as Antoine-Henri Becquerel and his photo plates in the context of the discovery of radioactivity, and Alexander Fleming and his yeast mold in the context of the discovery of antibiotics. The numberless instances of this general phenomenon show that luck is not only a prominently operative factor in such explicitly chancy matters as gambling or risk-taking entrepreneurship but that it also plays a significant role in such thoroughly rational enterprises as scientific inquiry. And there is no reason for disparagement here. After all, serendipitous discoveries are still discoveries.

Luck and Knowledge. Epistemic luck is not confined to science but is a general phenomenon. Convinced that Kate is next door, you claim: "I know that there is a tall woman in the next room." But unbeknownst to you, Kate has left the room and Sheila, who is also tall, has entered it. Is your claim correct? Your belief is true all right—no question about it. But the fact at issue—that there is a tall woman in the next room—and the ground for your belief in it (namely, that it is Kate) have become totally disconnected. It is only *by accident* that your belief is true. To be sure, this is not good enough for actual *knowledge*, as this term is generally understood. To constitute genuine knowledge, beliefs must not just be true—they must be properly grounded as well.

Isaac thinks that there is a dog outside because he believes he heard Rover bark there. But unbeknownst to him, Rover went inside and another dog came along. Isaac is cognitively lucky in that his otherwise plausible belief is also correct: there is indeed a dog outside. But, nevertheless, given his misimpression, we would not in this circumstance credit him with really *knowing* that there is a dog out there.[3] Usually and in the general run of things, a plausibly exposed true belief represents knowledge. But this is a rule that has exceptions. For when the grounding of that belief goes awry—as it can readily do in situations where bad luck becomes a spoiler—then the belief's truth is simply unable to redeem it as a view of real knowledge. For knowledge, it is not enough to have the correct answer by mere chance. If someone asks you for the (positive) square root of 81 and you respond 9 under the bizarre impression that square roots are calculated by summing up the digits involved (with $8 + 1 = 9$), the correctness of your response does not mean that you know the answer. Your correct answer did not reflect knowledge.

And much the same story also holds for rational prediction. Convinced that your brother will come home bringing his friend Rav Gandhi, you predict: "We shall have an Indian visitor here tomorrow." But your brother and his friend actually go to the museum instead, while nevertheless your friend Sin Singh drops by. Your initial prediction has come true all right, but we can hardly say that it has been fulfilled. For predictive correctness means that the grounds of the prediction and the facts that render it true must be in an appropriate alignment and coordination. In this regard correct prediction is a foreknowledge of sorts, and the entry of luck—"getting it right by a mere fluke"—is excluded. As with genuine knowledge, the element of proper understanding must be present in rational prediction.

The problem of knowledge is thus a complex issue. One way of reading the lesson urged by skeptics from classical antiquity to the present day is that no matter how conscientiously we "play by the rules" in matters of factual inquiry, there is no categorical assurance that we will answer our questions correctly. Even in science, there is an ineliminable prospect of a slip between evidence and generalization. But no less significant is the circumstance that, on the opposite side, there can also be epistemic windfalls: cases where we "play it fast and loose," as far as the rules are concerned, and still get our answers right. In managing our information as in managing other issues in this life, luck can become a determinative factor.

3. FORESIGHT VERSUS CHANCE IN HUMAN HISTORY

Is human history ruled by chance or by law? Is our human fate ultimately a matter of mere luck? Or was Hegel right and the real is rational? A long-standing and by now respectable tradition insists that a science of history is impossible. This is exemplified by the nineteenth-century German philosopher's bifurcation of the natural and the human sciences, with the former geared to predictions and control and the latter to understanding and explanation. And the human sciences were held to include not only the humanities (the "sciences" of human artifice) but also much or most of the social sciences (the "sciences" of human action). For—so it was argued— since people have free will, we cannot expect to achieve sure-thing prediction in the realm of human action; the most we can hope for is the exploitation of statistical trends and tendencies. And here we can never ensure the stability and fixity needed for more than highly conjectural prediction. In the domain of human action, science can underwrite plausible expectations but never secure forecasts.[4] And this means that luck is bound to play the decisive role.

Against this somewhat bleak assessment of the matter, there is another long-standing tradition that insists on the possibility of a science of human action based on the discovery of historical laws. Giambattista Vico, Karl Marx, Oswald Spengler, and, more recently,

Fernand Braudel all thought that a certain inevitability of natural process predetermined the future development of human society and civilization along foreseeable lines. For most of the classical theorists, the idea of historical predictability was closely bound to the idea of historical inevitability.[5] The question of historical prediction has usually been approached from the angle of some generalized theory of history that looked to the inexorable triumph of enlightened rationality, democratic egalitarianism, communistic socialism, material well-being, or the like. In particular, believers in inherent structural trends and tendencies of history have projected five major sorts of views:

- *progressive*: matters are moving to a new and totally different—and better—order of things (Enlightenment thinkers such as Edward Gibbon, Immanuel Kant, G.W.F. Hegel; progressive stage theorists like Auguste Comte; social evolutionists like Herbert Spencer; and social utopians such as Karl Marx, G. B. Shaw, and Edward Bellamy)
- *retrogressive*: matters are moving back to an older, earlier, and more primitive order of things (Max Nordau; fin de siècle theorists)
- *stabilitarian*: fundamentally things remain pretty much the same over the course of time (the "classical" position of those ancient and medieval thinkers who saw man as having a fixed nature and modus operandi; Arthur Schopenhauer)
- *cyclic*: historical change moves in a repetitive pattern of ebbs and flows (Ibn Khaldun, Giambattista Vico, Friedrich Nietzsche, Oswald Spengler, Arnold Toynbee)
- *anarchic*: historical change is wholly or at least predominantly a matter of haphazard eventuations that resist domestication to any sort of lawful regularity (Thomas Carlyle)

Among theorists of history, there accordingly developed a conflict between two dramatically opposed schools of thought. On the one hand the partisans of Destiny, who look to iron laws of historical development that canalize the course of history into an immeasurable and, in principle, foreseeable course. On the other hand stand the partisans of Chance, who envision sheer unfettered contingency—a flux of continual and impredictable chance, variation, innovation. The former school is convinced that the more fully we understand the world, the more clearly its fundamentally predictable nature will come into view. The latter believe that with fuller understanding comes a clearer view of the dominance of chance and contingency, which render history a fortuitous succession of "one damn thing after another." But here, as so often, the path of wisdom seems to run between the two extremes, with history seen as a tug of war between Destiny and Chance, where sometimes the one, sometimes the other, prevails.

To all appearances, then, the most plausible theory of the historical process is the doctrine of *punctuated chaos*, which sees the operation of a social system as a matter of periods of settled order and functional stability (within which prediction is possible) that are interrupted more or less at random (i.e., at unpredictable intervals) by chaotic transitions to a new, temporarily stable order. In such systems, short-term predictions are generally possible, but the longer range is generally intractable. And even in the context of a seemingly normal course of developments, unforeseeable and anomalous events can happen. (In the case of economics, consider the stock-market crash of October 1987 or the turbulent gyrations of the European monetary system in September 1992.) There is good reason to think that social systems of this world (economies included) function in exactly this mixed, halfway-house manner.

One contemporary informant tells us: "Many sociologists feel that not enough is known to predict future events."[6] But if this is indeed so, then these people are living in a world of hopeful self-delusion. For what impedes prediction in this domain is not a mere lack of information, a mere failure to develop the discipline as far as one can. Rather, the root cause is something very different, something that lies in the nature of the operative realities at issue. It is the nature of the phenomenology of the domain—its volatility, instability, and susceptibility to chance and chaos—that is responsible for our predictive incapabilities here rather than our imperfections as investigators.

Insofar as this view is valid, the great project inaugurated by Hegel of finding reason in history—and subsequently revamped by such twentieth-century history theorists as Spengler and Toynbee—seems destined to come to nothing. There is no inner unifying rationale to historical process—no unfolding of rational dialectic, no rhyme or reason, no way of eliminating the chance from the human scheme of things. There is no total escape from luck in this domain, only periods of comparative respite.

The most eloquent recent exponent of a theory of historical impredictability has been Karl R. Popper, who believes himself to have demonstrated that, "for strictly logical reasons, it is impossible for us to predict the future course of history" and who strongly criticizes the idea of discovering laws that underlie and determine the course of history.[7] Popper, in effect, views history as a succession of essentially unrepeatable processes whose characteristic idiosyncrasies mean that any theoretical generalizations about its course are untestable and thereby unscientific. The very idea of history as a social science is not only misguided but also objectionable in its commitment to a deterministic view of the human condition. (After all, as the example of political assassinations indicates, even small causes can produce vast and imponderable consequences in human affairs.)

Pejoratively characterizing as *historicism* the belief that secure prediction is possible in social and political affairs, Popper saw this position as quintessentially represented in the doctrine of Karl Marx. His prime reason for denying social predictability is straightforward: "Long-term prophecies can be derived from conditional scientific predictions only if they apply to systems which can be described as well-isolated, stationary, and recurrent. These systems are very rare in nature; and modern society is surely not one of them."[8] Popper insists that all "scientific" prediction from laws must for this very reason be limited to the case of a modus operandi that is secure against extraneous interference ("well-isolated"), grounded in stabilities ("stationary"), and classifiable in law-geared types ("recurrent"). Social systems do not satisfy these conditions—at any rate, not over substantial periods of time. In the context of agents interacting in the setting of human societies, human actions can and generally do have unforeseeable consequences. (There is, after all, no way of isolating a social system against the destabilizing impact of internal developments, let alone external ones.) The actions of human beings depend on their tastes and preferences and then are simply too volatile to provide for stable generalizations.[9] The difficulty with using even the best-established trends predictively is that "their persistence depends on the persistence of certain specific initial conditions."[10]

Overall, however, Popper pushed a sensible position too far. The problem is that a for-certain predictability is the only sort that Popper is prepared to contemplate in this context. He thus conflates predictability with necessitation. Now to reject a cast-iron historical determinism of the sort contemplated in Marxism is all very well. But to say without qualification that history cannot make any predictions at all is plainly false. We must, surely, differentiate between historical issues with respect to scale (the outcome of next week's mayoral election versus the development of the American novel) and also with respect to range (consumer attitudes in the next month or in the next century). Once such distinctions are heeded, it becomes clear that, on a sufficiently modest level, historical and social predictions are commonplace in modern life. Many safe predictions can certainly be made in the human domain, and many significant developments in human affairs can clearly be foretold with substantial accuracy, and there is little question that it is possible to make sure-thing predictions in the social sphere. For example: "Americans in the year 2500 will still be spelling 'and' as *a-n-d* and will not be adding a silent *e* at the end."

Again, take the proverbial death and taxes: one can safely predict that Bill Clinton won't be alive one hundred years hence and also that he will not effect a readjustment of the income-tax rate at zero. Much can be foretold on the basis of a historical analysis of past trends (e.g., demographic facts regarding life expectancies, population densities of cities and countries, or even such cultural phenomena as the number of scholarly books that will be published in a given country on a given subject-matter over the next five years). Barring major catastrophes, the number of a town's (or country's) third-grade school children next year is pretty well bound to approximate the number of second-grade school children this year.

The point is not that historical developments are unpredictable but that our prospects of successful prediction here are very modest—particularly with respect to those problematic issues that especially interest us. The sort of prediction we can achieve in this domain is not the kind that enables us to monitor the role of luck in human affairs. After all, the operation of choice, chance, chaos, and coincidence in the course of human events is so prominent that history is unable to provide for the reliable prediction of more than a minute fraction of those contingent developments that really interest us. What must be rejected is not so much *predictability* (à la Popper) as *fatalism*. (It is one thing to predict what you will do, given your tastes, disposition, and values, and something else—quite different—to predict what you *must* do, like it or not.) And, above all, it is very problematic to move from prediction—even of the fatalistically inevitable sort—to matters of social policy and praxis. Quite the reverse—those at issue do not need our help; if the victory of the proletariat were foreordained, there would be no need to go forth and urge people to bring it to fruition. If we were able to "replay" the game of human history up to any one particular point, we would almost certainly find that the detailed course of subsequent events soon diverges drastically from the actual course of things.[11] To all appearances, the hand of luck rests heavy on the shoulders of human history.

And the reason is not far to seek. Genuinely self-developing systems like human individuals and their societies contribute formatively to their own development. Their future is not preordained by their past. They manifest the operation of novelty, spontaneity, creativity. Such systems—be they biological, technological, or social—inevitably have aspects that are unpredictable because there are always some situations to which they make an ad hoc response and about which they simply "don't make up their mind until they get there," so to speak. It is here—in the sphere of authentic innovation and spontaneity—that we find the basic reason for the impredictability of many major historical developments.

We ourselves instantiate this phenomenon. The ever-changing nature of the human condition that results from ongoing innovation in virtually every relevant sector renders social, political, and intellectual laws difficult if not impossible to achieve at the level of historical significance. And, of course, where laws and lawlike regularities are unavailable, a scientific prediction of history's major eventuations thereby becomes unrealizable. Here the operation of chance comes to the fore. And so, where large-scale human issues are concerned, we have no choice but to acknowledge the power of Lady Luck.

VISIONS OF SUGARPLUMS

1. ATTITUDES TOWARD LUCK:
LUCK AS FRIEND AND FOE

It is a platitude that we live on borrowed time in this world. And the amount of credit extended to us in this regard is in substantial measure a matter of luck, seeing that the chance of disaster dogs virtually every step we take in a life where hazards confront us in immeasurable forms, from dangerous microbes to falling meteorites. We do not need to read the Book of Job to be reminded that a string of bad luck can sour the sweetest disposition; the daily paper serves perfectly well. Fortune can be very cruel—and so can our own malicious fellows. Sometimes the machinations of ill luck manage to turn the boon of life to ashes in people's mouths; as Plato's Socrates remarked, "it would be surprising if this one rule [that life is preferable to death] alone never had any exception—if it never occurred with men that, as in some other cases, it is better to die than to live" (*Phaedo*, 62A). The saying has it: "Call no man happy till he dies."

The bright side is more pleasant to contemplate. What makes luck so powerfully impressive a factor in human affairs lies in the fact that its workings go counter to life's "natural consequences." When an eventuation is lucky or unlucky, we do *not* "have it coming." It is little wonder that people naturally take special pleasure and joy in good luck, seeing that it brings us boons bestowed gratuitously by uncertain happenstance.

Mark Twain's Huckleberry Finn remarked acutely that we take

more pleasure in the dollar we find on the street than in the dollar we earn as a wage. The key here seems to lie in the familiar term Mother Nature. When luck comes our way, the world seems to smile at us with favor, giving us the reassuring sensation of being looked after by a kindly fate—the comforting sensation of being at home in a friendly realm whose controlling powers are concerned with our welfare. All depending on how people treat us, we will see them as enemies or as friends; and it is much the same with luck. When someone (correctly) realizes that he has been lucky, the natural reaction is one not only of surprise but also of delight. To receive a boon bestowed by fate—unbidden and unexpected—is something one is bound to find pleasant.[1] The work we do could have been done by *anybody*; but we are personally favored when good luck befalls us.[2] We see this as somehow pinning the world's Good Housekeeping seal of approval upon our humble selves.

But there are dangers here. Someone who views luck as a friend —who is fully persuaded that "luck is on my side"—is likely to rely on it too much, often to the detriment of a more productive reliance on his own efforts and energies. On the other hand, someone who mistrusts luck—who sees fate as a hostile conspirator and feels persecuted by an ill luck that will turn the best efforts into an exercise in futility—is hardly likely to put forth the effort and energy through which good results can generally be brought to realization in the ordinary course of things.

The path of human life is strewn with risks. Pretty much everything we try can turn out for ill as well as good. And a fog of unknowing—of inescapable impredictability—hovers all about us. Without some degree of optimism, life is unbearable. No human has the time, the fortitude, or the patience to take account of all the

103

things that might possibly go wrong. That matters will go well in ways we cannot exactly foresee is something we have to rely on every day of our lives. We do not and should not place an exaggerated reliance on luck, or "push our luck too far"; but without some hopeful expectation of luck, life as we know it would hardly be possible.

How should we shape our attitudes in the face of luck? What *should* we think about it? The cardinal rule is: *Think realistically*. With luck, as with most anything else, the course of reason is to recognize things for what they are. And since outcomes that are a matter of luck are (in the very nature of the case) unpredictable and uncontrollable, we cannot expect either to foresee or to control these issues. It makes no sense to "curse one's luck"—no one and no thing is responsible for it. And analogously, it makes no sense to be grateful for good luck. To be sure, one can be *happy* about it. But thankful? —No! Insofar as luck is—as it must be—the product of fortuitous chance, there simply is no one and no thing to bear responsibility for it. Unless we endorse a very strange theology, and see God as employing sheer accidents or opportunities for allocating rewards and punishments, it will make no sense to regard luck as betokening design.

When good or bad luck comes one's way, the sensible attitude is to "take it philosophically"—to take auspicious reversals of fortunes in stride, or, in the case of misfortunes, to steel ourselves to carry on the good fight on another field and on another day, remembering that "luck is bound to change." We have to accept luck for what it is—the unavoidable feature of a complex and frequently uncooperative world in which we operate beyond our depths, continually proceeding in the light of imperfect information about how matters will eventuate. One certainly can—and generally does—feel displeased and distressed by bad luck. Nothing is more natural. But it is never reasonable to feel affronted by it—to feel somehow mistreated. Such attitudes as offense, resentment, and the like are appropriate only for *deliberately* inflicted injuries. And this is emphatically *not* at issue with bad luck, which, by hypothesis, pivots on mere chance. To entertain the paranoia of maltreatment and persecution in this regard is as unreasonable as being angry and kicking the stool over which one has stumbled in the dark. When good or bad luck comes our way, the appropriate reaction is to accept it as "just one of those things" and come to terms with what cannot be helped. The rational stance is to avoid both the misguided euphoria of thinking that the world is on our side and the equally misguided paranoia of thinking that the world is out to get us.

The ineliminable role of chance in life means that how we fare is bound to be a mixture of skill and luck. And as concerns individuals—or, for that matter, groups—there is no fixed proportion between the two. It is instructive in this regard to contemplate the ramifications of optimisim and pessimism. Ms. Optimist counts on good luck. Just like Charles Dickens's Mr. Micawber, she takes the line that "something will turn up." She has no hesitation to run all sorts of risks, because she feels certain that luck will intervene to have everything come out right. She does not make elaborate plans and preparations, because she is convinced that luck will see her through. She lives in the present and lets tomorrow look after itself. (Americans are usually optimists, which helps to explain why the doomsday politics of the European "Greens" never took hold with us.) By contrast, Mr. Pessimist takes the gloomy view that "something is bound to go wrong." He cautiously avoids every avoidable risk because he counts on bad luck to make things go amiss. Neither approach makes good sense. Both kinds of errors betoken a counter-productive unrealism. The sensible view is clearly that of middle-of-the-road realism. The judicious thing to do is clearly to balance things out, to achieve a happy medium—to be prudently daring in taking risks so that the overall balance of the two sorts of bad luck is minimized. Ordinary prudence and good sense require a duly balanced intermediateness.

In shaping our attitude in the face of luck, the register of sensible precepts will prominently include the following:

- Be epistemically realistic! (Be realistic in your judgments.) Assess the probabilities and utilities at issue in life's eventuations by reasonable and subjectively cogent standards. Close—insofar as you can—the gap between the subjective and the objective by evaluating the probabilities and the utilities at issue in an appropriate way.
- Be practically realistic! (Be realistic in expectations.) Bear in mind that in situations of decision and action in the face of risks, you can do only so much and the course of reason is to do the best you can and rest content with that. The old Roman dictum that people have no obligation to do more than the best they can ("ultra posse nemo obligatur") still holds. We have to come to terms with the fact that in situations of chance and uncertainty, there is only so much one can do. "Don't fret what can't be mended."
- Be prudently adventuresome! Don't be so risk-averse as to lose out on opportunities. Calculate the odds and try to keep them on your side.
- Be cautiously optimistic! Do not let the prospect of failure in chancy situations prevent you from exerting plausible efforts in trying to bring a matter to a successful conclusion.

Luck, good and bad, is an ineliminable part of human existence. We have no real choice but to come to terms with it as best we can. The cardinal rule is to keep one's sense of proportion and not become unreasonably inflated by good luck or unreasonably deflated by bad. In particular, the course of reason is not to allow oneself to be defeated by bad luck but to persist in the face of inescapable adversity, to fight on, and to look to the brighter prospects of another day. Nor will it do, where others are concerned, to give undue credit or blame where what is at issue is no more than a matter of good or bad luck.

But what is the point of considering such wise counsels about luck if it is indeed true that their implementation calls for a realistic attitude? After all, people either do or do not have a realistic attitude, and if they do not, then they are not going to acquire it from reading good advice. There is, alas, a great deal of justice to this complaint. An intellectual virtue like realism is not obtained from written instruction. In this regard, realism and prudence, or conscientiousness, are in the same boat. Deliberations of the present sort may enable readers to *understand* the merits of a realistic attitude in the presence of luck, but will not necessarily lead them to *acquire* such an attitude. To this end, understanding is not enough; habituation is also called for. All that understanding can do is to supply reasonable people with an incentive.

2. THE PSYCHOLOGY OF LUCK

The natural reaction to having good luck is joy, pleasure, and at least concealed laughter. For the combination of surprise with the pleasure of a "happy" (i.e., fortunate) development is bound to produce amusement in anyone having even a modicum of "a sense of humor." On the other hand, someone else's having bad luck that is not *too* negative, combining a mild mishap with fortuitous unexpectedness (slipping on a banana peel, say), is also likely to engender laughter —though this time in others. For there remains in us still a remnant of that atavistic competitiveness that sees another's misfortunes as our own good.

For reasons somewhat difficult to fathom, empirical study of the psychology of luck is a rather underdeveloped domain. For example, we lack anything like a systematic study of people who have unexpectedly gained large fortunes (through speculation, say, or by an unexpected inheritance) or of people who have sustained unanticipated losses—those bankrupted in a stock-market crash, for example, or those who lose everything in a market collapse like the eighteenth-century South Sea Bubble or the post–World War I hyperinflation in Germany. However, anecdotal evidence does suggest that in the euphoria of large-scale good luck, people are likely to let their new-found wealth run out like sand between their fingers.

There is, clearly, a psychopathology of luck. On the one side we have the person who places an overreliance on luck. Such an individual is reckless by constantly "pushing her luck," doing foolish and imprudent things and counting on luck to come to the rescue. On the other side we have the paranoid individual who is convinced that the fates are against her and who, in an excess of caution, denies luck a fair chance by avoiding every avoidable risk, no matter how minor.

For some people "bad luck" unfortunately becomes an all-purpose excuse. As one nineteenth-century moralist put it:

Go talk with the mediocre in talents and attainments, the weak-spirited man who, from lack of energy and application, has made but little headway in the world, being outstripped in the race of life by those whom he had despised as his inferiors, and you will find that he, too, acknowledges the all-potent power of luck, and soothes his humbled pride by deeming himself the victim of ill-fortune.[3]

People of this inclination are ever ready to use bad luck as an excuse, portraying themselves as victims of circumstance instead of recognizing inadequacies of skill or effort and exerting themselves. Yet there is in fact little, if any, point in "cursing one's luck" when ill fortune befalls us. There is no sensible alternative to acknowledging the futility and wastefulness of a rage and resentment that impedes a constructive determination to work to shape matters in such a way that the likelihood of misfortunes and disasters is diminished.

These considerations have a decided bearing on the attitude that sensible people have toward luck. In particular, when you happen to have a run of good luck, you would do well not to preen yourself as a superior person who has somehow enlisted fortune's support. And if you have had a run of bad luck, you would be ill advised to retreat into your shell in the conviction that "the world is against you."

Above all, it is sensible not to come down hard on people who have bad luck, remembering that there but for the grace of luck and lot go you. It is folly to respond to other people's mere bad luck by fancying oneself superior. In general, when someone has bad luck, it makes no sense to "blame the victim." Nor does it make sense to respond to other people's good luck with envious resentment or jealousy.[4] Whenever life runs lotteries, *somebody* has got to win them, and it just joins misery to disappointment if you "eat your heart out" because victory did not happen to come your way. You are made into the person you are by what you do—by what you make of the opportunities that come your way. A healthy dose of realism is in order: you are not made either better or worse through good or bad luck.

Sensible people will, accordingly, avoid making a virtue out of chance and thinking that the lucky are somehow superior to those who are not and that the unlucky are somehow inferior. Insofar as it is indeed *luck* that is at work, the only difference between the lucky and the unlucky individual lies entirely in this circumstance alone. In the final analysis, there is no cogent reason to see this difference as indicating something deeper—some sort of virtue or defect of character or personality. Since luck is a matter of pure chance, a person's condition in this regard tells us *nothing* regarding her qualities.

3. LUCK AND WISDOM: THE PROVERBIAL PERSPECTIVE

The human and social sciences may have neglected luck, but this is certainly not the case with ordinary common sense. This fact is attested to by the frequency with which the term figures in proverbs and sayings.[5] We tend to resent the fact that "some people have all the luck." We remark that "people have to play the hand dealt them by fate" and note that "luck favors the well-prepared." We are apprehensive that "bad luck comes in threes." Then, too, luck figures in many things that we do. We "knock on wood" to ward off bad luck. We bet on our "lucky numbers," thank our "lucky stars," and carry a "lucky charm."

Proverbial lore stresses the power of luck—its ability to leap over otherwise insuperable-looking obstacles:

- Luck knows no limits.
- If you're lucky, even your rooster will lay eggs.
- If luck is with you, even your ox will give birth to a calf.

Precisely because luck is so changeable, we encourage people by saying, "Better luck next time," or "Never count luck out." Proverbial wisdom about luck sensibly directs us to the middle ground between the two extremes of over- and underreliance on luck, between placing too much trust in luck and underestimating its productive possibilities. Along the lines of the first we have many proverbs that warn against relying too much on luck:

- Don't push your luck.
- Never press your luck too far.
- Never trust to luck alone.
- You can never know your luck.
- Luck is always against those who rely on it.
- He has the luck of the Irish [but you're not Irish, so don't count on it].
- Lucky at cards, unlucky in love [so if you have luck in one area, don't count on luck's favor across the board].

Along the lines of the second extreme there are others, such as:

111

- The only sure thing about luck is that it will change [so if you've been "down on your luck" recently, don't despair: your luck will probably turn].

To be sure, proverbs tend to stipulate general rules, and in life all the rules have exceptions. Thus, taken too literally it is quite false that "good luck never comes too late." If you have recently been informed that you will shortly succumb to a fatal disease, there is little benefit to learning that you have just won the lottery.

A striking and significant feature of proverbial wisdom is its inconsistency, its Janus-faced tendency to look in opposite directions at once. As a variation of Newton's third law of motion, for every proverb of one tendency, there is another with equal force of the opposite tendency, as attested by the following pairs: He who hesitates is lost / Look before you leap. Beware of Greeks bearing gifts / Don't look a gift horse in the mouth. Look after the pennies and the pounds will look after themselves / You can't take it with you. Plus ça change, plus c'est la même chose / Tempora mutantar, nos et mutatur in illis. This changeability among proverbs marks the complexity of human life: that there is a time for prompt action ("A stitch in time saves nine") and a time for being slow ("Haste makes waste"); that "depending on conditions," both ways of proceeding are proper and well advised.

Naturally enough, luck also illustrates this tendency of proverbial wisdom to work both sides of the street. On the one hand we have:

- Luck is better than wisdom.
- Lucky men need no counsel.
- Good luck beats early rising.

112

All such proverbs stress the advantages of dumb luck over shrewd prudence. But, on the other hand, we also have:

• Luck favors the well-prepared.
• Bad luck is bad management.
• Diligence is the mother of luck.

The point, of course, is that we must both trust and distrust luck. We cannot, must not rely on it. And still we should not discount its potential altogether. Proverbial wisdom rightly speaks with forked tongue here.

4. LUCK AS AN EQUALIZER IN GAMBLING AND SPORT

Given the nature of the human condition, the prizing of luck is readily understandable. Only some of us are endowed with talent and natural ability. But anyone is potentially a recipient of luck. If I fancy myself winning in competition with a master player of tennis or chess, I am an idiot—in view of my lack of the requisite skills. But if I envision winning a lottery, I am no more foolish than anybody else. Anyone can carry off the prize here, and any person's chance of winning is just as good as anyone else's. Gambling of this sort is, in a way, a great equalizer. This goes a long way toward explaining both its popularity with people and its popularity with governments, for which such voluntary taxation is a close-to-ideal money-raising device.

We can all fancy ourselves lucky. The unrealism involved is perhaps fanciful but not altogether absurd. Moreover, with gambling we need not be so intimidated by bitter experience. Starting another business in the wake of a bankruptcy or another marriage in the wake of a divorce is indeed something of "a triumph of hope over experience." Not so with a lottery. My failure to have won the last time —or the last twenty times—does not mean that my chances of winning *this* time are in the least diminished.

In such gambling situations as lotteries, chance serves to eliminate the element of skill and clears the ground for pure luck. And even in mixed games of skill and chance—such as card games and various sorts of sport competitions—the presence of chance creates an element of suspense that adds interest to the venture. The role of luck in gambling and sports is accordingly a crucial one. Only where teams are rather evenly matched—where games are not too "one-sided," so that, given some "lucky breaks," either side can prevail—will a game or sport be of interest either for the participants or for the spectators.

The role of luck in the matter of gambling and gaming is something that deserves a closer look.

[VI]

THE PHILOSOPHERS OF GAMBLING

1. INTRODUCTION

The hope of gain, the thrill of suspense, and the proximity of kindred spirits—greed, boredom aversion, and human sociability—all draw people to gambling and ensure the persistence of this otherwise unproductive activity through every age.[1] But a deeper impetus also lies in the background here and betokens the symbolic presence of larger issues. For life, too, is in large measure a gamble —a game of chance, like roulette, rather than one of pure skill, like chess. The very words *luck* and *lot* link our topic to the theme of gambling.

Seeing that it pivots on the fortuitous, luck knows no law except the laws of probability. Probability theory provides our most effective available instrument for exact reasoning in those chancy and uncertain matters that delineate the natural habitat of luck. But how did it come to play this role? In an informative study of the origins of the mathematical theory of probability, Ian Hacking maintains that "the decade around 1660 is the birthtime of probability."[2] It was then that a calculus of probability was developed by mathematicians Pascal, Fermat, and Huygens, and others who addressed their efforts largely to problems of the division of gambling stakes. However, the period that immediately preceded this, the unsettled era of the Civil War in England and the Thirty Years' War on the Continent, had already witnessed a new concern on the part of philosophers with gambling, gaming, and the role of chance, accident, fortune, and luck in human affairs. In this way, the intellectual climate of a *philosophy* of chance set the stage for the development of the *mathematics* of chance. Only after matters of chance attracted the attention of moralists and philosophers—who now resumed under new conditions the ruminations about chance, fate, and fortune inherited from classical antiquity—did intellectual preoccupation with chance pass into the hands of the mathematicians, who revolutionized thought on the subject by developing the "calculus of chance" that we now characterize as the theory of probability.

In exploring this historical dimension of our topic, it is instructive to consider the ideas of four very different thinkers working in four substantially separate parts of Europe: Gataker, Gracián, Pascal, and Leibniz, working in London, Madrid, Paris, and Hannover, respectively.

2. FOUR THEORISTS

Born in London and educated in Cambridge, Thomas Gataker (1574–1654) was, for a time, preacher to the society of Lincoln's Inn.[3] He was a versatile scholar and influential Puritan divine who was nevertheless one of the forty-seven London clergymen to sign the address of January 18, 1649, against the trial and execution of the King. His 1652 edition of the works of Marcus Aurelius was described by Henry Hallam as the "earliest edition of any classical writer published in England with original annotations."[4]

In 1619 Gataker first published his tractate *Of the Nature and Use of Lots*.[5] The topic was apparently put on the agenda of the day by the great lottery of 1612, described in Stow's *Annales* as follows:

The King's maiestie in speciall favor for the present plantation of English Colonies in *Virginia*, granted a liberall Lottery, in which was contained five thousand pound in prizes certayne, besides rewards of casualtie, and began to be drawne in a new built house at the West end of *Paul's*, the 29th of June 1612. But, of which Lottery, for want of filling uppe the number of lots, there were then taken out and throwne away three score thousand blanckes, without abating of any one prize; and by the twentieth of July all was drawne and finished. This Lottery was so plainely carryed, and honestly performed, that it gave full satisfaction to all persons. *Thomas Sharpliffe*, a Taylor of London, had the chiefe prize, *vis.* foure thousand Crownes in fayre plate, which was sent to his house in very stately manner: during the whole tyme of the drawing of this lottery there were always present diuers worshipfull Knights and Esquiers, accompanied by sundry graue discreet Citizens.[6]

Gataker's book, however, does not focus exclusively upon lots and lotteries, but takes gaming in general into its purview, a lot being construed very generally as an event whose outcome is due to chance.

Gataker's treatise was a work of substantial erudition, running to over three hundred pages. It comprised an elaborate survey of historical examples of the use of lots in the Old and the New Testaments, for example: in the selection of a successor to the apostle Judas;[7] in the assignment of priesthoods and public offices in Greece; in the allocation of benefits in Hebrew, Greek, Roman, and other legal practices; in customs governing the division of booty and the spoils of war; and the like. (All four gospels state that the Roman soldiers used lots to divide the garments of Jesus.[8]) Gataker defined a "lot" as an "event merely casual purposely applied to the deciding

117

of some doubt" (p. 9), "casual events" being "such as might fall out in like sort diversely, and are not determined by any art, foresight, forecast, counsel, or skill of those that either act in them, or make use of them" (p. 14). He quotes with approval the dictum that "chance is founded, and dependeth upon Man's ignorance" (p. 37).

Gataker follows Thomas Aquinas in dividing the use of lots into the *divisory*, for effecting distributions or allocations of goods or evils; the *consultory*, for settling on courses of action or determining matters of fact;[9] and the *divinatory*, for seeking the will of God or the decrees of Fate as to what will happen in the future. Despite the common use of lotteries to finance charitable causes, Gataker limited his approval to their divisory role. The use of lots to divide the land of Israel (Numbers, 26:52–56) was, after all, expressly commanded by God (Gataker, p. 14ff.). Granting that God knows the outcome of lots (Proverbs, 16:33), Gataker rejected and criticized the view that "a Lot discovereth to men God's hidden will" (p. 25), arguing that "Lots are not to be used in [a] question of Fact past and gone . . . for what is no ordinarie Lot is able to decide; but where some question is who has the right to a thing; in which case, notwithstanding the Lot is not used to determine who in truth hath right to it, but who for peace and quietnesse sake shall enjoy it" (p. 148). Accordingly, Gataker insisted that, "concerning the matter of business wherein Lots may lawfully be used, the rule of Caution in general is this, that Lots are to be used in things indifferent onely" (p. 125), for,

> many good things there are that may at sometime be done, where of a man may made choice whether of them hee will doe, being not necessarily tied unto, or enjoyned any of them: As for

a student having divers bookes about him in his study, it is indifferent to choose one, this or that, refusing the rest, for present employment, there being no special occasion to urge the use of one more than another: Or for a man that carrieth a pair of knives about him, it is indifferent to draw and use either when occasion requireth (as Plutarch says, *De Stoicorum contradictiones*, 128).

As Aquinas observed, Augustine had maintained, "If, at a time of persecution, the ministers of God do not agree as to which of them is to remain at his post lest all should flee, and which of them is to flee, lest all die and the Church be forsaken, should there be no other means of coming to an agreement, so far as I can see, they must be chosen by lot."[10] Gataker agreed that it should be decided by lot who should "retire and reserve themselves for better times: that so neither those that stayed might be taxed of presumption, nor those that returned themselves be condemned for cowardice" (p. 66).

Poor Gataker! In the wake of his book, his promising clerical career was put in jeopardy by accusations that he favored games of chance.[11] This charge was certainly unjust. For Gataker's thesis was merely the employment of random-selection devices as a means of resolving matters of choice in cases where some preferential selection is desirable "for peace and quietnesse sake." Often, after all, lots are used in a perfectly harmless way—for example, in matters of divisory allocation, like the assignment of starting positions in swimming or rowing races (Gataker, p. 119). Moreover, as the Bible notes, "The lot causeth contentions to cease, and parteth between the mighty."[12] (A modern example of the sort of thing Gataker had in mind is afforded by the circumstance that when Hawaii was admitted as the fiftieth state of the Union and two new senators were elected conjointly, random devices were used by the Senate to decide which of the two would have seniority, with the decision made by a coin toss, and which would serve the longer term, with the decision made by card drawing.[13])

In Chapter 10, "Of Extraordinary or Divinatory Lots," Gataker expatiated against the use of lots "either for the discovery of some hidden matter past, or present or for the presaging and fortelling of some future event." The ensuing chapter argues at length that this sort of thing is superstitious and unlawful. However, other uses of lots can, in principle, be appropriate.

Gataker's position closely paralleled that of Cicero's *De divinatione*. There, Cicero approved the use of divination, and especially of augury, as a practice that had certain social and political benefits in fostering cooperative action and communal solidarity, and not at all because it had any prophetic utility—any predictive efficacy.[14] Cicero distinguished between an inappropriate (superstitious) use of signs, auguries, and portents for making informative prognostications about the future and an appropriate use of them for making communal *decisions* in controversial matters. The latter purpose promoted the preservation of public peace, since the authorities were relieved of the burden of choosing between the pro-faction and the anti-faction forces; the politically inexpedient matter was put "in the lap of the gods."

For the sake of fairness and impartiality, people want to be assured that human desires and predilections do not influence the exercise of official choice. The use of lots clearly is an effective way to attain this objective. And it was in this spirit that Gataker sought to maintain the principle that there is nothing heretical or immoral in the

120

use of lots per se. In the realm of human affairs, we sometimes want assurance that things occur "by chance" rather than "by design," and the use of lots is simply a way of insuring this neutrality.

However, in the last third of this treatise, Gataker ventured upon more dangerous ground. He suggested that games of chance can (and should) be harmless playthings. Gaming had its "lawful use" for diversion—good recreations—as well as its "unlawful abuse" (p. 194):

> But is it one thing to play at dice or cards and another thing to be a Dicer or Carder; as it is one thing to *drink wine*; and another thing *to be a wine drinker* or, as we use [sic] to say *a wine bibber* [p. 229].

Provided people do not overindulge in such diversions to the point of neglecting their business, and do not gamble for money, no harm is done. "Play [is to] be used as play; for pleasure, not profit; for game, not for gain" (p. 251). It was doubtlessly this part of his discussion that led Gataker into difficulty with his pious critics.

The very fact that Gataker had to defend himself against the charge of favoring games of chance testifies to a rising concern with gambling, which religious people have generally regarded as not only a manifestation of private inprudence and time wasting but also a mode of immorality and even impiety, because gambling abandons the use of God-given reason and bases a decision on the mediation of chance or fate.[15] Indeed, there is something impious about thinking that there are any "casual" or "chance" occurrences. It is only from our human point of view that "casual events" exist at all; an omniscient God keeps track not only of the flight of sparrows but of the toss of a coin as well. Despite his contention that chance has a useful role as an issue-settler in human affairs, Gataker was at one with his theological critics in believing that God does not play dice with his world.

A very different and far more favorable view of gambling and its analogy to life was taken by an important Spanish moralist contemporary with Gataker. Baltasar de Gracián y Morales (1601–58) was a theologian and philosopher who was educated in Toledo and entered the Jesuit order there as a novice at the age of eighteen. He published his books under the name of Lorenzo Gracián, prudence advising pseudonymous publication to deflect disapproval by the ecclesiastical authorities of discussions rather worldly for a priest.

Gracián's *Pocket Oracle* (*Oráculo manual y arte de prudencia*), first published in 1647, was a series of three hundred pithy precepts, each accompanied by a brief commentary, setting out the guidelines of prudent action. The book enjoyed a great popularity, was echoed by La Rochefoucauld, and admired and translated into German by Schopenhauer.[16] In this work, Gracián depicted the human situation as an analogy with card games and formulated practical advice on this basis. His position in this regard stood as follows:

In this life, fate mixes the cards as she lists, without consulting our wishes in the matter. [sec. 196]

And we have no choice but to play the hand she deals to us. But the wise man bides his time and places his bets when conditions are favorable. [sec. 163]

He tests the waters, as it were, before getting in too deep, and if matters look inauspicious withdraws to play again another day. [sec. 139]

The sagacious gambler never counts on luck's lasting and prepares for adversity amidst good fortune. [sec. 113]

There are *rules* for coping with risks and the sagacious person can facilitate good fortune. [sec. 21]

Of these rules the most important is to play well whatever hand fate may have dealt. [sec. 31]

Another cardinal rule is to know when to quit: the knowledgeable gambler never "pushes his luck." [sec. 38]

Thus one crucial rule is not to deem oneself as destined for domination. To think oneself to be the ace of trumps is a fatal flaw. [sec. 85]

In this way Gracián analogized the conduct of life to card play and reinterpreted the guidelines of good card sense as principles of life. As he saw it, life and playing cards are both games of chance, and the precepts for effective operation in both contexts are fundamentally akin. What Gracián's insight as a moralist properly brought to notice is that the good card player is not necessarily the one who is big. (That depends too much on luck.) Rather, it is the one who makes the best and the most of the cards he is dealt. And just here the deep analogy to life emerges. For the critical issue is once again clearly that of the quality of performance—of what we make of the opportunities that chance and circumstance put at our disposal.

Gracián's perspective struck a resonant note among his countrymen. Gambling has long been a prominent facet of Spanish life. (The *Lotería Nacional*, established by Carlos III in 1763, is the oldest continuous national lottery.) Official estimates indicate that money spent in gambling currently amounts to some 15 percent of family income, making Spain a world leader in this regard.[17] Spaniards have long tended to view gambling not as a human weakness or vice but as a plausible opportunity for improving one's condition.

The general attitude and outlook of Gracián's book accordingly made a substantial impact on Spanish philosophy, which has long resisted the northern European tendency to rationalize human affairs. And there is further good reason to see this as unsurprising. For while the Western philosophical mainstream has striven to imbue our understanding of the world with the intelligible order of a rational system, the Spanish philosophers of the anti-scholastic tradition have generally viewed the world as an uncertain, unpredictable, and unreliable setting for human life. Their position runs roughly as follows: Nature and we humans conspire in creating a difficult and largely intractable environment. Spanish philosophy has tended to keep reason in its place. It inclines to see reality, or at any rate that part of it that constitutes the setting for human life, as chaotic, incoherent, pervaded by disorder. Life is precarious. In all our doings and dealings, we cannot count on things going "according to plan." Planning, prudence, foresight, and the like can doubtless help to smooth life's path, but they are far from sufficient to ensure a satisfactory outcome of our efforts. Chance, accident, and luck—fortune, in short—play a preponderant and ineliminable role in human affairs. In all our doings and undertakings, we humans give hostages to fortune. The outcome of our efforts does not lie in our control: fortune (chance, contingency, luck) almost invariably plays a decisive part.

This fortunism did not, however, carry Spaniards to the extreme of an un-Christian fatalism. They were not drawn to the endorsement of inaction, lethargy, and a supine resignation to the inevitable. In their view, active enterprise is called for because our actions set the stage for luck: someone who does not play cannot win the game. To a degree—although a very limited degree—people are the authors of their own fortune. Although fortune disposes, man nevertheless proposes.

The changeable and unpredictable nature of the human situation means that flexibility and adaptability are major human virtues. People have to be many-sided, able to adapt to changing circumstances. Like a good actor, a successful person must be prepared to play very different parts. (Spanish literature offers the influential model of *el picaro* as a chameleon, a person who manages to attune himself to the requirements of the moment and is able to be all things to all people.)

On this basis, versatility and adaptability were seen by the Spanish anti-scholastics from the time of Gracián onward as crucial aspects of prudence. People whose lives are too orderly—who place too great a reliance on the regularity of an established system—thereby risk disaster. The sagacious man is one who has the prudence to develop this flexibility to accommodate himself to difficult and changing conditions. He strives to be able to emulate the Abbé Sieyès, a political theorist at the time of the French Revolution, who, when asked about his activities during the heyday of Robespierre and the Terror, responded, "J'ai vécu (I lived)."

In this way, Spanish philosophers took the prominence of fortune in man's affairs to betoken the limits of human power, setting the stage for a fundamentally pessimistic appreciation of the power of human reason in this sublunary sphere. We find this attitude conspicuous not only in the great figures of the Golden Age of Spanish literature, who were more or less contemporaries of Gracián (in particular, Quevedo and Calderón), but also in later ones, such as Unamuno, who insisted that human reason is inadequate and unsatisfactory as a guide to life, and Ortega y Gasset, who rejected the utility of scientific reason as director of human affairs. The idea that life is too chancy and fortuitous a thing to be managed by rational means runs as a recurrent leitmotiv through the history of Spanish thought. Gracián's recommendation of the gambler's perspective fell on fertile ground among the people of a society drawn to cultivating the prospects of good luck.

The life-is-a-gamble aspect of Gracián's thought was stretched to its ultimate limit by the French scientist and polymath, Blaise Pascal (1623–62). Though he died at the early age of thirty-nine, Pascal's many-sided genius flowered early, and despite the brief span of his life he managed to make an astonishing array of contributions in mathematics, physics, philosophy, and theology. His *Pensées* (*Thoughts*) was a collection of brief notes and drafts jotted down during the years 1657 through 1662 in preparation for writing an *Apology for the Christian Religion*. Published after his death, Pascal's *Pensées* enjoyed great popularity and has proved to be a work of enduring value and tenacious popularity.[18]

Pascal saw the role of chance in human affairs as pervasive:

Everyone ponders how best to make the best of his condition, as for the choice of condition and country, chance [*sort*, destiny] gives them to us. It is a pitiable thing because they have been taught that this is best. And it is this that determines each to his condition of locksmith, soldier, etc. [no. 98][19]

Change and caprice pervade human affairs. "Truth on this side of the Pyrenees, error on the other" (no. 294). In living this life, we constantly "take our chances." And this holds with regard to the next life as well.

In one brief passage of two sheets that form part of Pascal's rather haphazard assemblage, he presented his famous wager in favor of the religious life. It was addressed to his former fashionable friends, such as the clever but somewhat shady Chevalier de Méré, a typical worldly *libertin*: "Brilliant talker, fearless freethinker, and inveterate gambler."[20] The core of the wager argumentation ran as follows:

> When there is an equal risk of winning and of losing, if you had only two lives to win, you might still wager; but if there were three lives to win, you would still have to play (since you are under the necessity of playing); and being thus obliged to play, you would be imprudent not to risk your life to win three in a game where there is an equal chance of winning and of losing. But there is an eternity of life and happiness. That being so, if there were an infinity of chances to which only one was in your favor, you would still do right to stake one to win two, and you would act unwisely in refusing to play one life against three, in a game where you had only one chance out of an infinite number, if there were an infinity of an infinitely happy life to win. But here there is an infinity of an infinitely happy life to win, one chance of winning against a finite number of chances of losing, and what you stake is finite. That removes all doubt as to choice, wherever the infinite is to be won, and there is not an infinity of chances of loss against the chance of winning, there are no two ways about it; you must risk all.[21]

Recognizing the extent to which gambling had become fashionable among his worldly compatriots, Pascal seized on an ingenious scheme to capitalize on this phenomenon for apologetic purposes. His wager

argument, designed to accomplish its work by using the latest intellectual technology in deploying the machinery of mathematical
expectations, represents Pascal's enduring contribution to the development of probability theory, for a new mode of thought had entered
upon an old arena of discussion. "St. Augustine had seen that one
labors under uncertainty at sea, in battle, etc. But he did not see the
law of chance [*la règle des partis*, 'rule of partition'] which shows how
one ought to proceed."[22]

This is not the place to enter into the complexities of Pascal's
analysis. Suffice it to observe that, in effect, the wager discussion
says: "When gambling, you people act on the sensible principle of
evaluating wagers by blending the chances of an outcome with the
gain to be realized. Be consistent and do the same in matters of
religion. You will then have to agree that no matter how small you
deem the chances of God's existence, the infinite reward that will
come to the faithful, should He exist, serves to render the gamble of
religious commitment worthwhile." Pascal's famous wager argument
is, in fact, an invitation to think about the big issue of life in this
world and the next in the manner of a gambler.

As Pascal saw it, our very lives are a risky gamble that puts us at
the mercy of luck. As he trenchantly put it: "You find yourself in this
world only through an infinity of accidents" ("Vous ne vous trouvez
au monde que par une infinité de hazards"). "Your birth is due to a
marriage, or rather a series of marriages of those who have gone
before you. But these marriages were often the result of a chance
meeting, or words uttered at random, of a hundred unforeseen and
unintended occurrences."[23]

His work on games of chance made Pascal one of the founding
fathers of the mathematical theory of probability, for Pascal and his

coworkers managed the enormous achievement of imposing some degree of mathematical intelligibility on inherently fortuitous occurrences. His wager argument—which turns on using the machinery of mathematical expectations to assess the acceptability of gambles—was an ingenious use of a mathematical resource for the purposes of religious apologetics. Pascal marks the point of transition in which the philosophy of chance gives rise to the mathematics of chance. With the rise of probability theory, Pascal and his mathematical congeners discovered something that even the cleverest intellects of classical antiquity would have viewed as a virtual contradiction in terms—the existence of *laws of chance*.[24]

As this sketch indicates, our three theorists present a picture of rapid escalation. Gataker was concerned merely with defending the religious and moral legitimacy of a recourse to chance for resolving a limited range of practical issues. In Gracián, we find the idea of using the ground rules of gambling as guiding principles for the conduct of our everyday lives. With Pascal, we have the application of the principles of rational gambling as a basis for decision in matters of religion, governing our view of God and the life to come.

In the next generation, too, philosophers continued to devote attention to games of chance, with mathematician-philosopher-polymath Gottfried Wilhelm Leibniz (1646–1716) as the most prominent example. Leibniz was deeply concerned to deny that there is any room at all for chance on the stage of the world's events and processes. His basic ideological commitment was exactly that of Einstein: God does not play dice with the universe. A "principle of sufficient reason" was, accordingly, one of the cornerstones of Leibniz's philosophy, and he insisted time and again on "the great . . . principle that *nothing takes place without a sufficient reason*," in other words,

129

that nothing occurs for which someone who has enough knowledge of things cannot give a reason adequate to determine why the matter stands as it does and not otherwise.[25]

Leibniz saw the ultimate reason for all of the world's arrangement to lie in the will of God, and here, in the domain of God's will and choice, there is no room for any element of chance:

If the will of God had not as its rule the principle of the best, it would tend towards evil, which would be worst of all: or else it would be indifferent somehow to good and to evil, and guided by chance. But a will that would always drift along at random would scarcely be any better for the government of the universe than the fortuitous concourse of corpuscles, without the existence of divinity. And even though God should abandon himself to chance only in some cases, and in a certain way (as he would if he did not always tend entirely towards the best, and if he were capable of preferring a lesser good to a greater good, that is, an evil to a good, since that which prevents a greater good is an evil), he would be no less imperfect than the object of his choice. Then he would not deserve absolute trust; he would act without reason in such a case, and the government of the universe would be like certain games equally divided between reason and luck.[26]

Leibniz thus held that God always proceeds rationally, and rational choice must (by definition) proceed in line with principles of reason. Indeed, this holds for any genuine act of will:

In things absolutely indifferent there is no (foundation for) choice and consequently no election or will, since choice must be founded on some reason or principle. A mere will without

130

any motive is a fiction, not only contrary to God's perfection but also chimerical and contradictory, inconsistent with the definition of the will.[27]

To be sure, we humans can sometimes reasonably effect selections by random mechanisms such as lots, but only because our imperfect knowledge allows ignorance of outcomes:

But, as I have declared more than once, I do not admit an indifference of equipoise, and I do not think that one ever chooses when one is absolutely indifferent. Such a choice would be, as it were, mere chance, without determining reason, whether apparent or hidden. But such a chance, such an absolute and actual fortuity, is a chimera which never occurs in nature. All wise men are agreed that chance is only an apparent thing, like fortune: only ignorance of causes gives rise to it.[28]

Of course, such a selection does not qualify as a genuine *choice*: with us, as with God, rational choice must be based on reasons.

Leibniz was greatly interested in games of chance and gave much encouragement—and some active help—to the development of the theory of probability.[29] He saw the development of the formal theory of games of chance as useful to the human intellect and peculiarly suited to its powers (specifically as a rational means for reflecting our intellectual deficiencies). But putting *epistemological* consideration aside, Leibniz's *metaphysical* concern was precisely to deny any room for considerations of chance or probability in the ontology of the real. For Leibniz, metaphysics must approach the issue from an omniscient point of view, and at *this* level there is simply no place for chance or probability, since a benevolent God would not and does not "play games" with his creation. The opponents of Gataker worked to exclude gambling from England; Leibniz and his followers worked more ambitiously to exclude it from nature.

For Leibniz, there can be no such thing as real, ontologically grounded chance in this world, where all eventuations are preprogrammed. There is merely epistemic chance, grounded in the imperfections of human knowledge. It is thus something reducible and removable to the extent that human knowledge can be improved, and elsewhere rationally manipulable insofar as the calculus of probability can be applied.

And so, the developments of a calculus of chance in the seventeenth century was limited to an optimistic expectation that luck could be domesticated to reason. The fathers and godfathers of probability theory saw it as a guide to the tactics of sagacious gambling, and, by analogy, they further saw in the tactics of sagacious gambling a guide to the rational conduct of life in an uncertain world. Accordingly, they believed that the rational domestication of chance made possible by the calculus of probability could in its turn produce a mechanism for the rational management of luck.

What these seventeenth-century theorists tried to do is to shift the topic of chance from the realm of the occult to the sphere of scientific understanding. Theirs was the hubris of seeking to domesticate chance to the operations of reason—to contract radically the scope of luck in the management of our affairs in a chancy world by conquering for the goddess of wisdom, Athena, much of the terrain of the goddess of luck, Fortuna.

3. THE ETHOS OF THE ERA

Just what is it that accounts for the philosophers' concern, from 1610 to 1650, with gambling and games of chance? The answer lies in the prominence of gaming in contemporary European society, a phenomenon that was itself largely the consequence of the troubled, wartime conditions of the day.[30] In fact, gambling has generally acquired particular popularity in periods of social chaos.

The turbulent era of the Civil War in England and the Thirty Years' War on the Continent witnessed a gambling epidemic across Europe. It began among soldiers and sailors who needed to kill time during long periods of enforced inactivity away from the more varied and constructive activities of civilian life. An anecdote from the Thirty Years' War related by the Spanish soldier of fortune Alonso de Contreras (1582–ca. 1641) illustrates this phenomenon:

After the capture by us Spaniards of a moorish ship in the Mediterranean had produced much booty, the commander of the victorious galleon, knowing well the predilections of his men, strictly forbade gambling, so that each soldier would preserve his share and return to Malta a wealthy man. To enforce this order, he had all dice and cards thrown overboard. But the urge to gambling among his men was not to be so easily denied. They drew a chalk circle on the deck and each concurrently placed a louse near its center, the winner to be whose louse first crossed the line and left the circle. Great sums were wagered on this basis. When the commander learned of this, he let his men have their way, recognizing that this vice of gambling cannot be suppressed among soldiers.[31]

Whenever life is cheap and hard—as it certainly was for seventeenth-century soldiery—gaming and gambling becomes a prospect whose attractions follow only a short distance after those of drinking. The civil military authorities of the period struggled in vain to contain gambling among soldiers. All attempts to prohibit or restrict it ultimately came to naught.[32]

The prolonged crisscrossing of the Continent by the armies and military hirelings of the major powers during the Thirty Years' War thus led to a diffusion of gambling throughout Europe. The mania for gambling soon spread from the soldiers to civil society in general—polite and otherwise.

It is little wonder that *casino* (Italian diminutive for *casa*, a house) became in the seventeenth century the name for a place of public amusement at pleasure resorts, where concerts, theatrical performances, and public balls were given, and where there was also usually a café-restaurant and—more relevantly to the present purpose—a gaming saloon. Initially, the gambling mania pervaded France, Spain, and the Netherlands,[33] but it crossed the Channel to England as well, moving with the return of the exiled court from the Paris of the Chevalier de Méré to the London of the Restoration. The Gaming Act of 1665 (16 Car. II. c.7), directed "against deceitful disorderly and excessive gaming," was the first piece of English legislation to regulate gambling debts.[34] (Persons winning more than one hundred pounds on credit were not only prohibited from recovering the excess but subjected to penalties for winning it.)

The most graphic description we have of gaming in this period is from Samuel Pepys, and it is well worth quoting at length:

[Went] to see the manner of the gaming at the Groome-porter's [the controller of gaming at court] . . . where . . . they begin to play at about 8 at night—where to see how differently one man took his losing from another, one cursing and swearing, and another only muttering and grumbling to himself, a third without any appearing discontent at all—to see how the dice will run good luck in one hand for half an hour together—and another have no good luck at all. To see how easily here, where they play nothing but guinnys, 100 pounds is won or lost. To see two or three gentlemen come in there drunk, and putting their stock of gold together—one 22 pieces, the second 4, and the third 5 pieces; and these to play one with another, and forget how much each of them brought, but he that brought the 22 did think that he brought no more than the rest. To see the different humours of gamesters to change their luck when it is bad—how ceremonious they are as to call for new dice—to shift their places —to alter their manner of throwing; and that with great industry, as if there was anything in it. To see how some old gamesters, that have no money now to spend as formerly, do come and sit and look on; as among other, Sir Lewes Dives, who was here and hath been a great gamester in his time. To hear their cursing and damning to no purpose; as one man, being to throw a seven if he could and failing to do it after a great many throws, cried he would be damned if ever he flung seven more while he lived, his despair of throwing it being so great, while others did it as their luck served, almost every throw. To see how persons of the best quality do here sit down and play with people of any, though meaner; and to see how people in ordinary clothes shall come hither and play away 100, or 200 or 300 guinnys, without any kind of difficulty. And lastly, to see the formality of the Groome-porter, who is their judge of all disputes in play and all quarrels that may arise therein; and how his

135

under-officers are there to observe true play at each table and to give new dice, is a consideration I never could have thought had been in the world, had I not now seen it. And mighty glad I am that I did see it; and it may be will find another evening, before Christmas be over, to see it again; when I may stay later, for their heat of play begins not till about 11 or 12 o'clock; which did give me another pretty observation, of a man that did win mighty fast when I was there; I think he won 100 pounds at single pieces in a little time; while all the rest envied him his good fortune, he cursed it, saying 'A pox on it that it should come so early upon me! For this fortune two hours hence would be worth something to me; but then, God damn me, I shall have no such luck.' This kind of profane, mad entertainment they give themselves. And so I having enough for once, refusing to venture, though Brisband pressed me hard and tempted me with saying that no man was ever known to lose the first time, the devil being too cunning to discourage a gamester; and he offered me also to lend me ten pieces to venture, but I did refuse and so went away.[35]

In the reign of Charles II, gambling was all the rage at court, and its fashionableness helped to spread it widely through town and country. Pepys was shocked at finding that even Sunday was not respected at court. On February 17, 1666/7, he writes: "This evening going to the Queen's side to see the ladies, I did find the Queen, the Duchess of York, and another or two at cards, with the room full of great ladies and men; which I was amazed as to see on a Sunday, having not believed it, but contrarily, flatly denied the same a little while since to my cosen Roger."

In fact, women were at the forefront of fashion here. On February

14, 1667/8, Pepys observed: "I was told to-night that my Lady Castlemaine is so great a gamester as to have won £15,000 in one night, and lost £25,000 in another night at play, and has played £1,000 and £1,500 at a cast." The niece of Cardinal Mazarin, who came over to England and was a favorite of Charles II, was an avid gambler. She won 1,400 guineas from Nell Gwyn at basset in one night, and over £8,000 from the Duchess of Portsmouth, "in doing which she exerted her utmost cunning, and had the greatest satisfaction, because they were her rivals in the royal favour."[36]

In theory, the probability calculus could have arisen in a very different way, one that had nothing to do with games of chance—from the rationalization of insurance, for example, or from the need for mathematical expectations in legal contexts of inheritance.[37] But, in fact, its actual impetus came from games of chance.

In the seventeenth century, then, gaming and gambling pervaded the soldiery of Europe and thereupon diffused through society at large. Having first drawn the notice of the upholders of discipline and good order in the military services, games of chance soon attracted the attention of philosophers and moralists, and then, finally, that of the mathematicians. In the order of historical causes and effects, the mathematical calculus of probability can be traced to the gambling mania of the soldiers of the Thirty Years' War.

An instructive symbolism is at work in this conjunction of events. Indulgence in gaming and gambling paradigmatically illustrates the irrational side of human nature, since placing one's hard-gained resources at risk on the throw of a die or the draw of a card may be viscerally thrilling but may wittingly and deliberately hand one's fate over to circumstances wholly beyond one's control. The great faith of seventeenth-century philosophers in the power of reason to illumine and improve the condition of man—present throughout such otherwise varied thinkers as Hobbes, Descartes, Spinoza, and Leibniz—is symbolically validated in the creation of a "calculus of chance," which manifests the capacity of reason to establish a base in the very heartland of its most powerful enemy, the sphere of chance and random contingency. Philosophical contemporaries saw the origins of the calculus of probability as a powerfully encouraging sign of the capacity of human reason to master the vagaries of uncontrollable circumstance.

Unfortunately for this optimistic vision, however, the light of further reflection and the lessons of bitter experience led to an eventual disillusionment. Applying the calculus of probabilities requires first mapping out the spectrum of possible outcomes. Only then can one gather adequate statistics for obtaining meaningful probability values for effecting those calculus-guided calculations. But in a domain where novelty, innovation, and surprise is prevalent, this essential precondition cannot be met. Probability theory unquestionably represents our best effort at the rational taming of luck. But in a sphere where there is much uncertainty about the nature of the prevailing situation and vast ignorance as to the very possibilities for the future, the calculus of probability is unable to operate effectively.

The rational domestication of luck is a desideratum that we can achieve to only a very limited extent. In this respect, the seventeenth-century philosophers of chance were distinctly overoptimistic. For while probability theory is a good guide in matters of gambling, with its predesignated formal structures, it is of limited usefulness as a guide amid the greater fluidities of life. The analogy of life with games of chance has its limits, since we do not and cannot effectively play life by fixed rules, a fact that sharply restricts the extent to which we can render luck amenable to rational principles of measurement and calculation. And here the moral dimension of the matter looms into view.[38]

VII

THE MUSINGS OF MORALISTS

1. OWING TO LUCK'S CHANCINESS, FAIRNESS DOES NOT ENTER INTO IT

Could all of a successful person's achievements arise through sheer luck? In theory, it is certainly possible. But it is also very unlikely. The world as experience reveals it to us is simply not so user-friendly that all kinds of actions—well-considered as well as heedless, careless as well as careful—will come out all right. Things can sometimes turn out well despite folly or incompetence. But one should not count on it. One should not "push one's luck." People can indeed be lucky. But somehow or other, it is generally not we ourselves but somebody else who manages to be the beneficiary of undeserved boons.

It is a natural if somewhat lamentable human reaction to resent and envy the good luck of others—to be jealous of the unmerited good fortune that comes their way. After all, there is, by hypothesis, no good reason why they should fare better than we do in the circumstances—why, say, *their* lottery ticket should gain the prize and not *ours*. And even if we are sufficiently urbane to suppress jealous and envious sentiments, nevertheless, the most rational and realistic among us cannot wholly avoid regretting that we do not live in a world ruled by reason—a fair world in which there is a just equilibration of fate and desert.

Spinoza thought that rational people would become resigned to the world's adversities by seeing them as the products of an inexorable necessity. But this is deeply problematic. For such a conviction cannot eliminate that nagging doubt from the back of our minds: just why should it all be strictly necessary—why should what actually happens be inevitable in the large scheme of things? (What would go so wrong with the world "if I were a rich man," as the protagonist asks in *Fiddler on the Roof*.) Such doubt is irremovable. And there is nothing intrinsically absurd about feeling put upon by an unkind necessity.

But mere chance does differ from necessity in this regard. For, by its very nature, it leaves no room for reasonable complaint on grounds of unintelligibility. Once it is recognized that chance is at work, no *further* accounting can reasonably be expected. A rationalization in terms of chance and luck will satisfy all *reasonable* demands here exactly because it is final: insofar as those adversities and negativities indeed are the products of chance, that "why" question is entirely preempted. When we say that something is due to pure chance, the explanatory regress is thereby terminated, and the prospect of (and need for) any *further* explanation is automatically precluded. The regress of reasons is at an end. After all, if there were some deeper reason why a generally fortuitous occurrence eventuated so as to favor one party over another, then that outcome would—for this very reason—fail to be a fortuitous one, contrary to hypothesis.

Do people deserve their fate? When things go well or ill for them, do they "have it coming"? This is something that very much depends. When eventuations are the just rewards for the good actions of an agent, or the just penalties for the bad, then the answer is clearly yes. But life being what it is, there is something that all too often simply is just not so. The (somewhat misnamed) French writer Lesage (1668–1747) tells us in his novel *Gil Blas* that when something

141

bad happens, "look to yourself and you will always find that it is at least partly your own fault" ("examinez vous bien et vous verrez qu'il aura toujours un peu de votre faute"). The twentieth century with its world wars and its holocausts has made a mockery of this contention, though the wars of the Fronde should already have put Lesage on notice.

The Book of Job offers us an eloquent and heartfelt disquisition on the unmerited misfortunes that can befall good people. And no reader of newspapers is unaware of the reverse phenomena—the innumerable cases where the good things of this world fall to the lot of the bad. For luck by its very nature is a matter of haphazard. It does not require any profound exposure to the ways of the world to see that good fortune and luck do not generally favor the deserving, and the reverse the undeserving. The Amerindians of Peru, for example, did nothing whatever to invite the ominous risks that the coming of the conquistadors brought upon them; they were simply unfortunate. And what here holds for the fate or destiny of people holds for their luck as well. Experience shows all too clearly that "life is unfair"—and luck is one of the prominent reasons why. What actually happens to us in life is often a product of haphazard and chance, of good or bad luck, "of circumstances beyond our control."

The world's happenstance distributes the good things of this world (wealth, good looks, musical talent) in a decidedly uneven way. Ordinarily there is a bell-shaped distribution of worldly goods: a comparatively few people are given a markedly superior allocation, a comparatively few come up decidedly short, and the great majority fall in between—neither significantly below the mean nor significantly above it. Those who fall at the extremes—who are markedly underprivileged or markedly overprivileged in these regards—are fortunate or unfortunate as the case may be. And in general it is simply "fate" or "destiny" that decides, since the benefit or negativity at issue is (by hypothesis) neither due to any accomplishment or failing on the individual's part nor transpires through the individual's doing something to bring that benefit or negativity upon himself.

With matters of luck the whole idea of fair/unfair simply does not apply, because fairness is excluded in the nature of the case. A person can no more be fairly or unfairly lucky than she can be cleverly or uncleverly lucky. If cleverness came into it, it wouldn't be a matter of luck. And the same holds for fairness. Luck is something chancy, and chance by definition excludes cleverness, fairness, and similar bases of rationalization. Someone can deserve a piece of good luck, but it never comes his way *because* of that fact.

You bet a dollar on the outcome of a coin toss. There is, of course, no special merit in winning and no special demerit in losing. The issue is not a matter of desert at all. Where chance or unforeseeable haphazard is at work, outcomes (by hypothesis) have no deeper meanings. Luck, be it good or bad, is no index of worth but only the product of chance, accident, or unforeseeable haphazard. And it only makes sense to feel vindication or guilt in response to things for which we are responsible. Thus, when bad luck comes our way, there is no *rational* basis for resentment, since it only makes sense to feel victimized if what happens is the product of someone's malignity. Thieves and vandals do us deliberate damage, but tornadoes and earthquakes, which may do just as much harm, are no more than "tough luck." Such impersonal privations (which only a character assassin could call acts of God) can be regarded as deliberate victimizations only by those who are prepared to see the impersonal workings of nature through the crimson-colored glasses of a persecution complex.

It lies in the fortuitous nature of luck that desert has nothing to do with lucky and unlucky eventuations. People may be deserving of the good or bad things that luck brings their way, but it lies in the nature of things that they are never lucky or unlucky *because* they deserve it. Good luck often comes to the unworthy; ill luck to those who deserve better. (If lotteries were destined to be won by the most deserving, they would be selling a lot fewer tickets.) But when genuine *luck* with its inherent admixture of impredictability and fortuitousness is at issue, then it would always be a mere superstition to contemplate the matter in causal terms of reward or retribution—to think that people come by their good or bad luck because they somehow deserve it. Luck, be it good or ill, generally comes to people not only uninvited but also unmerited.

The fortuitous lacks all rhyme or reason. It is simply folly to think that chance seeks us out for reward or punishment, praise or reproach. To be sure, the idea has been current ever since antiquity that the gods speak through randomness—that the drawing of lots or straws reveals the resolution that is right and proper in the cosmic scheme of things.[1] The idea is that the outcome selected by such a random process is not just random but somehow contrived by the world's governing powers—that what is at work here is not just luck but a divine plan of some sort. People's instinctive disinclination to concede that portentous developments may be due to pure chance renders them unwilling to accept the surd as such, and leads toward the superstitious supposition that reason somehow lurks behind the workings of a merely apparent chance. But all this is no more than gross error and superstition. No one deserves credit for good luck or blame for bad. Seeing that luck is in its very nature something that lies outside an agent's sphere of control, it lies outside the realm of her responsibility as well. Otherwise, the duly cautious admiral whom a stray shot removes from the scene of battle—say, Nelson at Trafalgar—certainly would be blamable for leaving his fleet in a leaderless lurch.

In general, there is nothing else, nothing further and deeper and more far-reaching that we can say once we have remarked that people have been lucky or unlucky. We *cannot* emphatically say that they deserved it, asked for it, had it coming. Eventuations attributable to luck are—by hypothesis—outside the domain of intentionability. And this fact makes them ineligible for appropriate reactions of guilt or resentment. Seeing that people's luck is fortuitous—a matter of the world's chance and chaos that permits of no deeper rhyme or reason—there is nothing we can do to explain or rationalize luck, and nothing to warrant praising or condemning its recipients. When we have said that the eventuation was lucky or unlucky, we have said it all.

One cannot properly appreciate the human realities so long as one labors under the adolescent delusion that in this life people get the fate they deserve. During every century of the existence of our species, the planet has borne witness to a measureless proliferation of unmerited human suffering and a cruelly unjust maltreatment of people by circumstance and by one another. Only in exceptional circumstances is there any linkage between the normative issue of the sorts of people we are and the factual issue of how we fare in this world's course of things. The disconnection of the two factors of fate and desert, which luck so clearly signalizes, is a fact of life—a perhaps tragic but nevertheless characteristic and inescapable feature of the human condition.

2. THE POLITICAL ECONOMY OF LUCK AND THE ISSUE OF COMPENSATION

Nobody says that the world is fair. Life is not a level playing field. Some get to sit on thrones, others to languish in a terrorist's hideaway—and generally there is no cogent qualification test either way. And as with fate, so with luck. Merit and desert have little or nothing to do with it. Where the workings of luck are concerned, the modern passion for justice is bound to be disappointed. There are no entitlements for luck. When someone is "down on his luck," then if it is indeed luck—the mere chance of things—that has produced these unhappy circumstances, then the unfortunate at issue clearly deserves our sympathy and consideration. But does he also deserve our aid? Luck's inherent unfairness clearly opens the way to the idea of balance and compensation. Perhaps deliberate human intervention should set the balance right, restoring fairness where the world's haphazard has set the balance askew. The issue of the extent to which society should make up for the vagaries of luck in their impact upon its members is an interesting question of social philosophy.[2]

In some cases an adjustment is clearly feasible and perhaps also desirable. Affluent societies often compensate the victims of "acts of God" (floods, tornadoes, earthquakes) and sometimes those of various sorts of human malignity as well (riots, crimes of violence, etc.). But this process clearly has its limits—for one thing, by excluding the losses sustained by those who deliberately subject themselves to needless risks. Then, too, the widespread practice of a special tax on windfalls and treasure troves could be seen as a venture in enabling society-at-large to profit by the good luck of some. But here again, there are reasonable limits. One would hardly want to penalize elsewhere the fortunate high school graduate who is lucky enough to have his application accepted by the "college of his dreams." But, of course, the question remains of where those limits lie. How far is it reasonable to go in this direction?

One widely respected ethicist tells us that in a just social order the disparities inherent in circumstances of birth will be redressed in various regards: "since inequalities of [inherited] wealth and natural endowment are undeserved, these inequalities are to be somehow compensated for."[3] Presumably this would be done by improving the lot of the unfortunates rather than by leveling everyone else down to their condition. And, of course, society already takes some steps in this direction by such measures as inheritance taxes and welfare benefits for those born blind or crippled. Yet would it make sense to compensate children for the indifference or incapacity of their parents? And would we want to compensate people for a lack of good looks, talent, ambition?

Compensation for the negativities of fate and fortune can go only so far. And the situation is similar with luck. Certain particular sorts of bad luck no doubt can and should be compensated for by a sufficiently affluent society:

• loss by "acts of God": earthquakes, storms, floods, natural disasters
• loss due to unavoidable occasional malfunctions in the operation

of a public infrastructure resource (the vehicular traffic system, the air transportation system)
• loss by warfare, civil riot, terrorism, criminality

There may well be good, pragmatic reasons why an affluent society should compensate the victims of such sorts of socially or environmentally rooted bad luck—though clearly there is only so far a society can and should go in this direction, limits being set by both considerations of practicability and considerations of desirability. Social policy considerations of the usual kind are at work here. And the operative guiding principle should be: (1) that the person involved sustains an individually unforeseeable though statistically predictable loss, (2) that such loss is sustained in a way in which the victim bears no substantial personal responsibility, in that the issue lies outside the range of her effective control, and (3) that considerations of significant public advantage are involved.

The fact remains that compensation can—even in theory—make only limited inroads upon the power of luck in life. Luck's complex and vast impact on human affairs precludes effective manipulability. There is simply no way of leveling the playing field of life. Indeed, efforts in this direction are in good measure inherently self-defeating. In trying to compensate people for ill luck, we would simply create more scope for luck's operation. For whatever forms of compensation are adopted—money, increased privileges, special opportunities—the fact remains that some people are in a far better position to profit by them than others, so that luck expelled by the front door simply reenters by the back.

The impracticability of leveling the playing field of luck inheres in its utter unrealism—the fact that such a project lies beyond the possibility of human attainment. In view of the immense variety of ways in which good and bad luck can come people's way, there simply is no workable way in which one could compensate people for their bad luck. Chance is too variable and many-sided a factor. Would we even want to try to offset the influence of luck in human risk-taking ventures—in gambling, in marriage, in business ventures? Clearly, to try to do this even in small measures would be to transform the conditions of social life— to say nothing of effecting an absurd and totally ill-advised transfer payment from the prudent people of this world to those who are foolhardy. Should we as a society even try somehow to compensate people for the innumerable negativities that sheer chance brings their way: catching cold, missing their connecting flights, getting burgled, being abandoned by a fickle spouse? Even raising these questions brings a smile, because the list is, in principle, unending. Moreover, it is by no means clear that everyone would welcome such compensation. Many of us would look joylessly on the agents of the Commissariat of Equalization, come to inform us of our penalties for our good luck in recovering some stolen property—or in wooing and winning a talented spouse. There is simply no practical way to iron the wrinkles of luck out of life's fabric by compensatory arrangements.

While social utopians would fain compensate for this world's unfairness of fate and luck, philosophers, characteristically less sanguine, have generally looked elsewhere for compensation—to the next world of the church fathers, the unending, temporal long run of Leibniz, or the noumenal order of Kant. Such recourse to a region beyond that of present reality does at least betoken a sober recognition of the unavoidable role of luck in this world's scheme of things. For luck marks the deep conflict between the actual and the ideal in this world. The most needy and deserving people will not, in general, be the beneficiaries of good luck. Luck is the shipwreck of utopias—the rogue force that prevents ideologues from leveling the playing field of life. Only before God, the just law, and the grave digger is the condition of all alike and equal. Rationalistically minded philosophers have always felt uneasy about luck because it so clearly delimits the domain within which we humans have control over our lives.

3. LUCK THE LEVELER

While luck's impact means that life is unfair, there is, nevertheless, a more positive aspect to the matter. Luck is also a great leveler. Its very exemption from a subjection to reason works to make the playing field of life more level. Luck's abrogation of life's usual arrangements creates a situation where "everyone has a chance." It means that the race is not necessarily to the swift alone. The beautiful people—handsome, rich, well endowed by nature, and well equipped with the world's goods—can suffer the ravages of hard luck. And the world's victims—handicapped by the lack of life's good things—can have their bleak condition alleviated by spurts of good luck. Even proverbial wisdom recognizes that luck can compensate for a lack of natural advantages:[4]

- Good luck beats early rising.
- A pocketful of luck is better than a sackful of wisdom.
- Luck is better than science (or *wisdom*).
- You don't need brains if you have luck.
- Lucky men need no counsel.[5]
- Better born lucky than rich.

Luck brings surprises. It distributes favors and penalties in a basically fortuitous way. Even those blessed by fortune with great endowments may yet falter; even those who lack fortune's favor may "get lucky." Luck prevents life from being too rational and too predictable. Idealizing theorists say, "To each according to his abilities and efforts." But luck says, "Rubbish," and awards prizes of life's lottery as it lists. It mixes things up and adds to "the spice of life." The prospect of luck brings hope to the otherwise hopeless. And life being what it is, there is nothing worse than the destruction of hope.

Luck contributes to the leveling of life's playing field by creating a multitrack access to success, ensuring that ability and drive need not always prevail by giving some chance to the just plain lucky. The very destabilizing force of chance and luck serves to prevent the total domination by one category of the sort that moralists tend to favor —the deserving, the talented, the diligent. In this regard, luck is a great populist force that gives everyone a chance. (This perhaps serves to explain why moralists—who standardly incline to an elitism of the good—have generally taken a dim view of lotteries.) A world in which luck plays a role is not for this reason more *just*, but it is somehow far more *democratic*—by widening the range of those who have a chance at the good things of life to include *everyone*.

But perhaps luck is at odds with morality at an even deeper level?

4. CAN ONE HAVE MORAL LUCK?

To all appearances, luck affects not only our material condition in life in point of wealth and fortune but also our moral condition.[6] For, to all appearances, the moral status of otherwise identical actions can seemingly be at the mercy of luck. Consider the case of the lucky villain who burgles the house of his grandfather, whom he knows to be absent on a long journey. Unbeknownst to him, however, the old gentleman has meanwhile died and made him his heir. The property he "steals" is thus his own—legalistically speaking, he has in fact done nothing improper; a saving fluke has averted the legal wrong his actions might otherwise have committed. In his soul or mind—in his intention—he is a wicked thief, but in actual fact he is quite guiltless of wrongdoing, since his act was one of "taking something that belongs to oneself." Seemingly his moral standing has been saved by a piece of good luck.

By contrast, consider the plight of the hapless benefactor. To do a friend a favor, he undertakes to keep her car while she is away on a long journey. Toward the expected time of her return, the car is reclaimed by the friend's scheming identical twin—of whose existence our good-natured helper has no inkling. With all the goodwill in the world, he has—by a bizarre act of unhappy fate—committed the misdeed of giving one person's entrusted property over to another. In intention he is as pure as the driven snow, but in actual fact he has fallen into wrongdoing. To all appearances, a piece of bad luck rather than any flaw of character has made a malefactor of him.

Such cases illustrate how, to all appearances, the moral status of actions can be at the mercy of fortuitous circumstances. And it was, in fact, considerations of exactly this sort that led Immanuel Kant to put such moral accidents on the agenda of ethical theorizing. He insisted that with moral agency the rationale is pivotal. As he saw it, *moral* status and stature are wholly determined by what one wittingly endeavors to do and not by one's success, or actual performance. And there is much to be said for this view.

Consider the case of a bank's night watchman who abandons his post of duty in order to go to the aid of a child being savagely attacked by a couple of men. If the incident is "for real," we see the night watchman as a hero. However, if the incident is a diversion stage-managed as part of a robbery, we might well consider the night watchman to have been an irresponsible dupe. And yet from *his* point of view, there is no visible difference between the two cases. How the situation turns out for him is simply a matter of luck.

In this way various courses of action seem—to all appearances— to acquire a moral status that depends largely or wholly on how matters happen to turn out, which is generally something that lies largely or wholly outside the agent's sphere of control.

But is it actually so? To clarify the matter, let us now shift attention from action to character and consider moral qualities in the abstract. Character traits—moral ones included—are dispositional in nature, relating to how people *would* act in certain circumstances. For example, candor and generosity represent morally positive dispositions; dishonesty and distrust negative ones. But note that a person can be saved from the actual consequences of malign dispositions by lack of opportunity. In a society of adults—in a mining camp, or on an oil rig—the child molester has no opportunity to ply his vice. Again, the very model of dishonesty can cheat no one when, Robinson Crusoe–like, he lives shipwrecked on an uninhabited island— at any rate, until the arrival of man Friday.

Perhaps all of us are to some extent in this sort of position—are moral villains spared through lack of opportunity alone from discovering our breaking point, learning our price. As Schopenhauer somewhere observed, the Lord's Prayer's petition "Lead us not into temptation" could be regarded as a plea for matters so to arrange themselves that we need never discover the sorts of people we really are.

But what, then, of the moral position of the individual who is venial by disposition and inclination, but has the good fortune to be able to stay on the good side of morality because the opportunity for malfeasance never comes his way? As one recent discussant insists, "If the situation never arises, he will never have the chance to distinguish or disgrace himself in this way, and his moral record will be different."[7] But this being so, must morality not let such a blackguard off the hook entirely, since the issue of opportunity lies beyond the agent's control and "it seems *irrational* to take or dispense credit or blame for matter over which a person has no control"?[8] Plausible though this may sound, it gets the matter badly wrong. The difference between the would-be thief who lacks opportunity and his cousin who confronts and seizes it is not one of moral condition (which, by hypothesis, is the same on both sides); their moral *record* may differ, but their moral *standing* does not. From the vantage point of one who "sees all, knows all" by an insight that penetrates into a person's depths, the moral status of the two individuals would be the same. The morally lucky culprit is lucky not because his moral condition is superior but simply because he is not unmasked. The difference here is not moral but merely epistemic. Lacking the occasion to act, he cannot be found out as being what he actually is. (With the merely would-be wrongdoer, we cannot, of course, deplore the *act* which never occurred, but we can and must, by hypothesis, deplore the moral condition of the individual.[9])

The role of luck in human affairs has the consequence that the lives we actually lead—including all the actions we actually perform—need not in fact reflect the sorts of persons we really are. In the moral domain, as elsewhere, luck can obtrude in such a way that, be it for good or for bad, people simply do not get the sort of fate they deserve. And this specifically includes our moral fate, too—for good or ill we may never be afforded the opportunity of revealing our true moral colors to the world at large, and indeed may even be spared from confronting them in the painful light of personal recognition. Where we are lucky, however, is not in avoiding the stigma of wickedness but only in avoiding exposure.

The "morally lucky" villain is not, in fact, *morally* lucky (by hypothesis, he is a villain), but is *socially* lucky only because that reprehensible nature is not disclosed to the community. The difference is *not* one of morality; it is a matter of not being found out, of "getting away with it." It is precisely because both one's *opportunities* for morally relevant action and (unfortunately for the utilitarianism of John Stuart Mill) the *actual consequences* of one's acts lie beyond one's own control that they are not determinants of one's position in the eyes of morality. Most recent discussions of "moral luck" fail to appreciate the fact that the opportunity-deprived immoralist's good luck appertains not to his *moral status*, but merely to his *reputation*. He is, by hypothesis, a moral reprobate and is lucky only in not being found out as such. (Of course, we have no alternative—given the difficulties of epistemic access—to forming our judgment of people on the basis of what we observe them saying and doing. But all that is mere *evidence* when the moral appraisal of human agency is at issue.)

On this issue, Kant was entirely right: someone who is prevented by lack of opportunity and occasion alone from displaying his cupidity and greed still remains at heart an avaricious person and (as such) merits the condemnation of those right-thinking people who are in a position actually to know this to be so—if such there are. What ultimately

155

matters for the moral dimension is not achievement but endeavor. How people think and how they are determined to act are even more crucial for moral evaluation than what they actually manage to do. And it is exactly this that prevents luck from being a crucial factor here. We would do well to see luck as an extraneous factor that does not bear on the moral condition of a person's actions and character in other than evidentiary regards. And we hold people responsible for their moral character, not because we believe that they somehow chose it for themselves but because taking them as they indeed are is part of the fundamental moral presumption involved in treating a person as a person. People's moral attributes do not come to them by luck but emerge from them as free individual agents. Holding people responsible for their moral character (rather than seeing this as something added fortuitously *ab extra*) is part and parcel of the fundamental moral presumption involving treating a person as a person. To see this as an extraneous addition that may or may not come one's way by luck is simply to cease to treat people as people.

This helps to explain why it is that while someone who suffers from some physical disability can plausibly excuse himself from (say) a rescue effort by pleading his condition, the immoralist cannot comparably plead *his* natural inclinations and tendencies and look to his innate cupidity, avarice, lecherousness, or the like to get him off the moral hook. For in such a case it is exactly his disposition that earns him disapproval. The fact that he did not come by his disposition by choice is immaterial; dispositions are by nature not the sort of thing that comes up for selection. After all, it makes no sense to say things like, "Wasn't it just a matter of luck for X to have been born an honest person, and for Y to have been born mendacious?" For it is exactly those dispositions, character traits, and inclinations that constitute these individuals as the people they are. One does not choose one's character; it is one's character that makes one into the sort of person one is in the first place. We are not morally responsible for *choosing* our bad character (character is not the sort of thing that is up for choice); but we are morally responsible—and morally reprehensible—for *having* it. And here luck does not enter in. One can meaningfully be said to be lucky not in regard to who one is but only with respect to what happens to one. Identity must precede luck. It makes no sense to envision a prior featureless precursor who then has the good (or bad) luck to be fitted out with one particular group of character traits rather than another. With persons, as with objects of any sort, there is no appropriate place for "bare particulars" devoid of any and all descriptive properties. Identities are not allocated by a lottery of some sort to otherwise nondescript individuals.

To be sure, the point cuts both ways. The virtuous person can be preempted from any actual manifestation of virtue by uncooperative circumstance. Here is the moral hero primed for benign self-sacrifice—prepared at any moment to leap into the raging flood to save the drowning child. But fate has cast him into an arid and remote oasis, as devoid of drowning children as Don Quixote's Spain was lacking in damsels in distress. Of course, we would be unlikely to *recognize* this heroism in either sense of the term. On the one hand, we would be unlikely to *learn* of it. And on the other, we would—even if evidence did come unalloyedly our way—be ill advised to *reward* it in the absence of circumstances that brought it into actual operation. (For one thing, we would not be unalloyedly confident that it is actually strong enough not to break under the pressure of an actual need for its manifestation.) One's moral condition and status is something that lies within—in one's intentions, one's thought-life, one's inner nature and makeup. Fortuitous external events have no determinative role here. There is, in the final analysis, no such thing as *moral* luck. The very idea is a contradiction in terms that comes to grief in a dilemma. If the significant evaluation at issue results from luck, the morality does not enter into it. And if it is moral through being in some way within our responsibility and control, then it is not a matter of luck.

5. THE CENTRALITY OF THE ORDINARY

Does the potential gap between one's acts and one's moral condition mean (as Kant thought) that morality is not of the world—that moral appraisal requires making reference to an inaccessible noumenal order that stands wholly outside the empirical sphere of real life? Surely not! We must form our moral judgments not on the basis of what happens *transcendentally* in a reality-detached noumenal order but rather on the basis of that most prosaic of all suppositions —namely, that things happen as they *generally and ordinarily* do, that matters take the sort of course that it is only plausible to expect.

Moral evaluation as we actually practice it generally reflects the *ordinary* course of things. *Ordinarily*, breaking and entering is a wicked thing to do. *Ordinarily*, driving drunk increases the chance of harm to others. *Ordinarily*, mendacious people cause pain when they scatter lies about others. *Ordinarily*, people ultimately get to manifest their true colors. Moral appraisals are *standardized* in being geared to the situation of the common run of things. Admittedly luck, be it good or bad, can intrude in such a way as to prevent matters from running in the tracks of ordinariness. And then things go wrong. Moral acts that normally lead to the good can issue in misfortune.

But that is just "tough luck." It does not—or should not—affect the issue of moral appraisal.[10]

When someone's pet dog is killed by darting into the path of a car, the driver is not callous but just unlucky. When, heedless of possible pedestrians, a driver rushes out of an alley and happens to hit no one, this lucky result does not mitigate his moral culpability. Unlike legal culpability, moral blame or credit in such matters hinges on what can plausibly be expected and not on actual outcomes—or what actually chances to occur. It is this gearing to the issue of what can reasonably be expected to happen that detaches moral evaluation from the issue of actual outcomes in a way that factors luck out of the picture.

What is at issue here is a fact not so much about chance and luck as one about morality. For it lies in the nature of morality that luck cannot be a determinative factor here. Pure chance and unforeseen contingency cannot redeem an otherwise immoral act or make immoral an otherwise meritorious one. And since the *actual* consequences of our actions are at the mercy of chance, this means that a moral evaluation cannot be geared simply and solely to actual outcomes. What counts for morality has to be in the region not of *actual* outcomes but *expectable* ones.

Moral assessment pivots on what can reasonably be anticipated. People who drive their cars home from an office party in a thoroughly intoxicated condition, indifferent to the danger to themselves and heedless of the risks they are creating for others, are equally guilty in the eyes of *morality* (as opposed to *legality*), whether they kill someone along the way or not. Their transgression lies in their playing Russian roulette with the lives of others. Whether they actually kill someone or not is simply a matter of chance—of accident and sheer statistical haphazard. But the moral negativity is much the same one way or the other—even as the moral positivity is much the same one way or the other for the person who bravely plunges into the water in an attempt to save a drowning child. Regardless of outcome, the fact remains that, in the ordinary course of things, careless driving puts people's lives at risk unnecessarily, and rescue attempts improve their chances of survival. Someone who "gets away with it" is lucky all right, but not *morally* lucky. What matters for morality is the ordinary tendency of actions rather than their actual results under the unforeseeable circumstances that may occur in particular cases.[11]

One philosopher flatly denies this. Thomas Nagel writes:

> Whether we succeed or fail in what we try to do [in well-intentioned action] always depends to some extent on factors beyond our control. This is true of . . . almost any morally important act. What . . . [is accomplished] and what is morally judged is partly determined by external factors. However jewel-like the good will may be in its own right, there is a morally significant difference between actually rescuing someone from a burning building and dropping him from a twelfth story window while trying to rescue him.[12]

The difference he speaks of is indeed there. But only because of a lack of specificity in describing the case. Preeminently, we need to know *why* it was that our rescuer dropped the victim. Was it from carelessness or incompetence or a sudden flash of malice? Or was it because, despite all due care on his part, Kant's "unfortunate fate" intervened and a burnt-out timber gave way under his feet? If so, then Kant's assessment surely prevails.[13] Different circumstances may make for different evaluations. But where an agent's success or failure is differentiated only and solely by matters of pure chance, there is patently no reason for making different *moral* appraisals one way or another.[14] The person who runs afoul of her moral obligations to others without doing any actual damage is lucky all right, but not *morally* lucky. With morality, luck is out of the picture; strictly speaking, there simply is no such thing as *moral* luck.

6. THE PERSPECTIVE OF THE GREEKS

The Kantian perspective goes straight back to the Greek tradition. Greek moralists were generally attracted to the following line: How happy we are will in general be a matter of accident. *Happiness (hê-donê)* is chancy business; pleasure is bound to depend on circumstance and fortune—on the fortuitous opportunities that luck places at our disposal. If fate treats one adversely enough, then one may simply be unable to realize the condition of happiness (as counterdistinguished from rational satisfaction). Chance plays a predominant role here—circumstances beyond one's control can be decisive. But our *virtue (arêtê)* is something that lies within our character and thereby reflects our real nature. And this holds in general for the achievement of true well-being along the lines of the Greek *eudaimonia*. One is entitled to take rational satisfaction in a life lived under the guidance of sound values, irrespective of how circumstances eventuate in point of happiness.[15] Mere luck cannot create or destroy true values; it can neither make nor break merit.

The world—the real world that encompasses the contingency of chance, chaos, and choice—brings sheer luck on the stage in a way that disconnects actual fate from personal merit. And struggle as we will to set the balance even, the hard realities of an uncooperative world often condemn our best efforts to futility. The social values we prize—justice, fairness, etc.—are rightly esteemed by us, but that does not mean that we can bring them to actualization. We can, however, try; we can make the effort. And as Kant emphasized, morality depends on effort rather than success. One's affective *happiness* lies in the hands of the gods, but one's moral *goodness*—or one's *desert* for happiness, to put it in Kantian terms—is something that lies in one's own power.

Here Kant was surely right in following the lead of the Greeks. Morality as such is impervious to luck: no matter how things eventuate, the goodness of the good act and the good person stands secure from the vagaries of outcomes. But Kant's analysis of this situation went wrong. If morality prescinds from luck, this is not because morality contemplates the *ideal* situation of a *noumenal* sphere but because (as indicated above) morality contemplates the *normal* situation of the *ordinary course of things* in this mundane sphere of our quotidian experience—a course from which the *actual* sequence of events can and often does depart.

There is, to be sure, some good reason for viewing the failed and the successful rescue in a different light. For—by hypothesis—we know of the person who brings it off successfully that she has actually persevered to the end, whereas the person whose efforts were aborted by mishap might possibly have abandoned them before completion for discreditable motives such as fecklessness, folly, or fear. We recognize that an element of uncertainty pervades all human activities and that an uncharacteristic flash of inconstancy might possibly deflect someone in the process of performing a worthy act. But if we did somehow know for certain—as in real life we never do—that, but for circumstances beyond her control, the agent would indeed have accomplished the rescue, then we will have no basis for denying moral credit. Our reluctance to award full credit has its grounding in considerations that are merely evidential and not moral. On all indications, then, Kant's appraisal of the issue was quite right in *this* regard.

Thus, consider a somewhat variant case—that of the brave woman who leaps into the raging waters (or flaming inferno) to save a trapped child. Only after the fact does she learn that the child is her own. Had she known it all the time, she would indeed have got full marks for motherly solicitude—since in the circumstances we would have to presume that it was this, rather than disinterested humanitarianism, that provided the motive. But once we establish that she had no way of realizing this at the time, we have to award her full moral credit.

To be sure, the idea that intentions are paramount needs to be implemented with an admixture of common sense. For with a little novelistic imagination we can all envision bizarre circumstances in which the exercise of the standard virtues (truth telling, kindness, etc.) produces disastrous effects. But their status as virtues is geared to the ordinary course of things—how matters *standardly* and *normally* go in the actual world. It is because morality is geared to the world's ordinary course of things that heroic action is not a demand of morality but a matter of supererogation. (And it is this, of course, that is the Achilles' heel of Kant's analysis.)

It is in fact not difficult to construct examples that illustrate the advantages of the present normalcy-oriented approach as compared with Kant's noumenal perspective. Consider the case of Simon Simple, a well-intentioned but extremely foolish lad. Thinking to cure Grandmother's painful arthritis, Simon bakes her for twenty minutes at 400 degrees Fahrenheit in the large family oven. He labors under the idiotic impression that prolonged exposure to high temperatures is not only not harmful to people but actually helpful in various ways—curing arthritis among them. His *intentions* are nothing other than good. Yet few sensible moralists would give Simon a gold star. Simon falls down in handling a conflict of duty. In contexts of moral and rational decision, knowledge (intellect) matters as much as intention (will). We have a duty—especially where the stake is large —to inform ourselves adequately about the facts of the situation. It would not have taken much effort in this direction for Simon to correct his crazy misimpression. For he should know what any ordinary person knows: that broiling people medium-well by prolonged exposure to temperatures of 400 degrees is bad for them. In actual practice, we base our moral judgment on the ground rules of the ordinary case, and Simon's good intentions simply do not get him off the hook here. (That is just another aspect of his misfortune.)

The moralists of classical antiquity—and in particular the Stoics —grappled with the question: What assets of a person's endowment are secure against the ravages of bad luck? Clearly not wealth and reputation, which ill luck can all too easily destroy. And not even talent and ability, which can be negated by ill luck's denial of any and all opportunity for exercise and development. No, they insisted, only a person's inner nature—their character as defined by such moral virtues of honesty and good will, or such moral vices as the reverse—will represent positivities or negativities that cannot be damaged by ill luck. Moral virtues alone of human goods are not at the mercy of circumstances and are to be prized especially for this very reason. And their imperviousness to external circumstances and fortuitous developments means that they lie at the very core of what makes an individual into the person she really and truly and most deeply is. All else is a matter of what happens to one, but these character-instituting virtues and vices lie at the very core of one's being.

The person who defaults on a valid moral commitment (a promise, say, or an obligation of some sort) is not excused by a fortunate issue of this fault. A transgression whose unforeseeable consequence turns out to have a fortunate issue for those concerned (a *felix culpa*) is still a transgression. And the same holds for the morally virtuous act gone awry through the intervention of an unbound fate. Insofar as moral assessment is consequentialistic, it is geared to expectable, normal, standard, and foreseeable consequences, and not to the fortuitous issue of the individual case.

The artist who abandons his family to follow his guiding star, the father who sacrifices his child to the demands of his god, the statesman who breaks his word to his associates for the national good do not "violate pedestrian morality in the name of a higher *moral good*"—all allow extramoral objectives to override moral considerations. We may or may not decide to excuse them in so acting, on the basis of "everything considered." And we may, in the end, conclude that they acted "rationally" (i.e., for good and sufficient reasons). But we must not deceive ourselves into thinking that they acted *morally* after all—that their moral status as such is somehow safeguarded by their luck in realizing positive objectives of some sort. The mayor who fraudulently diverts money from the road repair fund to build a children's splash pool in the park may be a hero of sorts, but certainly not a *moral* hero.

What has been said here about the relationship of luck to morality holds for the relationship between luck and practical rationality as well. Even if performing a certain action is in fact conducive to realizing your appropriate ends (if, say, ingesting yonder chemical substance will actually cure your illness), it is nevertheless *not* rational so to act if you have no knowledge of this circumstance (and all the more so if such information as you have points the other way). Practical rationality (as distinguished from practical success pure and simple) requires due care for process. Even when we happen by luck or chance to do what is, in the circumstances, the best thing to do, we have *not* acted rationally if we have proceeded without good reason to think our actions appropriate—let alone if we had good reason to think they would be inappropriate. The agent who has no grounds for thinking that what she does conduces to her appropriate ends is not acting rationally. And this deficiency is not redeemed by unmerited good fortune—by luck's having it that things turn out all right. Rationality in action is not a matter of acting *successfully* toward our ends but one of acting *intelligently*, and given the role of chance in the world's events, these are not necessarily the same.

In sum, while the role of luck may be decisive for the *actual results* of our actions, it is not so for their *evaluative status*, be it rational or moral. We live in an imperfect world, where desert and result are all too easily disconnected. And the evaluative domain that includes both the moral and the epistemic spheres is by no means exempt from this general rule.

From the moral point of view, the crucial thing is to earn an E for effort. Whether our circumstances are straitened or easy, whether our childhood is protected or brutalized, whether our chances in life are many or few—all these are not a matter of our own choosing but lie "in the lap of the gods." But what matters from the angle of morality is what we make of the opportunities at our disposal, however ample or meager they may be. Of those to whom little is given, little can be expected, and of those to whom much is given, much.

166

Our horizons for moral action may be narrow or wide—that depends on the vicissitudes of facts. From the moral point of view, however, it is—to reemphasize—effort that counts. Those who confront a steep slope cannot be expected to make headway comparable to that of those who find an easy path before them. Situations and circumstances are realities of luck, but the rational evaluation of moral blame or credit is, of course, designed to take this into account. The crux lies in William James's injunction to the morally strenuous life, which would have us make the most of our opportunities for the good.

And there is no getting past the fact that sometimes the circumstances set the stage for tragedy. Consider the Black Death in the fourteenth century. The first attack of plague in the late 1340s carried off fifty thousand people in Paris—half the existing population. Grass grew in the streets and wolves attacked people in the depopulated suburbs. In enclosed places like monasteries, convents, and prisons, death was frequently total. Throughout Europe, Jean Froissart said, "a third of the world died" when the plague struck. With wars, famines, and brigandage contributing to the impact of the recurrent outbursts of plague, Europe lost half her population by the end of the century. Doomsday seemed to be at hand. Many, thinking the apocalypse to be in the process of enactment, believed that the end of the world had come and that humanity's future was over. Many— but not everyone. "In October of 1348, Philip VI asked the medical faculty at the University of Paris for a report on the affliction that seemed to threaten human survival. With careful thesis, antithesis, and proofs, the learned doctors ascribed it to a triple conjunction of Saturn, Jupiter, and Mars in the 40th degree of Aquarius said to have occurred on March 20, 1345."[16] But, clearly, herein lay hope. If a bad conjunction of the stars caused the disaster, a good conjunction could undo the damage. Petrarch wrote: "O happy posterity who will not experience such abysmal woe and will look upon our testimony as a fable."[17] When one survives a disaster of such a nature, it seems natural to ask the oppressive question: "Why am I one of the lucky ones—for what special mission was I spared?"[18] But if the matter is indeed one of chance, selection has nothing to do with it.

There is a serious accident—a plane crash, say, or a car crash. The circumstances are such that "by rights" (by ordinary expectation) everyone on board should have been killed. But Sally Smith walks away unhurt. She is obviously very lucky to have survived. And once she realizes what has happened, she will—or should—be surprised by this good fortune. Will she automatically be pleased? Almost certainly so. It is a perfectly natural and appropriate reaction. In the ordinary course of things, good luck will of course give us pleasure —particularly if we realize that it has not come our way at the expense of other people. But it is difficult to escape the *survivor syndrome* of "Why me?"—akin to its even more familiar distant cousin, the *victim syndrome*, which pivots on the same question. The survivor is likely to feel a special responsibility allied to guilt; the victim a special resentment allied to paranoia. The one carries with it an unfair burden of responsibility, the other an unfair burden of persecution. All this is natural enough. But, nevertheless, either sentiment is equally inappropriate from the rational point of view. When good luck comes our way, we will certainly be happy. But one cannot be literally *grateful*. There is no one—and nothing—to be grateful to. And the matter is certainly not one of having one's merits recognized.

In matters of sheer luck, where we are the beneficiaries or the victims of chance, that's simply the end of it. Where actual chance is at work, neither the fortunate nor the unfortunate are somehow selected for reward or punishment. The long and the short of it is that in human life as we actually live it there is no stable connection between the outcomes of our actions and our deserts: life is simply too chancy—too much of a lottery—to admit of harmonization here. In a realm of chance, people simply do not get the fate they deserve.

Influenced by the Stoics and the Epicureans, many among the ancients insisted that we ourselves are masters of our fate. But this is deeply problematic—unless we too agree in rejecting the impact of chance upon the human scheme of things. For the machination of chance and contingency means that we just are not the authors of our luck—let alone of our fate and destiny in this world. But the Stoics had a point. We are to a considerable extent the masters of our own spirit and personality—controllers not of what happens to us but of what we allow good luck and bad luck and fortune to do to us. We are not masters of our circumstances, but we are—or should be—masters of ourselves. How the world treats us lies largely beyond our control. But how we *deserve* to be treated is something that, in the final analysis, lies wholly within our power. Our fate is not within our power, but our character is. Luck manages to decouple fate from desert. But no force can decouple merit from desert.

Does good luck bring happiness? The question is not as easy as it looks. The proper answer pivots on various distinctions—in particular, those between objectively real and subjectively apparent luck and between affective and reflective happiness. Human psychology being what it is, the person who inadvertently gets what she wants is bound to be pleased. So, clearly, subjectively apparent good luck is more than likely to bring affective happiness (pleasure) in its wake.

And the person who gets what she actually and genuinely needs will, *if she realizes it and is rational about it,* take reflective satisfaction in this development. So objectively real luck will also bring reflective happiness (evaluative satisfaction) in its wake—albeit only when that italicized condition is satisfied. On the other hand, the contentions that apparent luck brings reflective happiness (rational contentment) or that real luck—which involves meeting genuine needs—brings us affective happiness (that is, pleasure) are both clearly false.

7. THE NORMATIVE DIMENSION

A general principle runs like a leitmotiv through deliberations on the bearing of luck on issues of morality. Acting morally—like behaving rationally or judging justly—is a normative matter that calls for proceeding correctly. And the normativeness at issue runs all the way through and *demands appropriate results appropriately arrived at* under conditions where chance severs the chain of appropriateness. To be sure, in all such matters the actual result is at the mercy of luck: it may be strictly by accident that we do the proper thing or give the right answer or reach the correct decision. But right action and rational belief and just judging involve more; above and beyond appropriateness of product, they demand appropriateness of process.

In strictly practical contents, getting the right result is enough; someone who has a practical problem—finding a lost book, for example, or finding his way out of a maze—is wholly successful even if he happens to hit on the right solution by pure chance. But in normative contexts such as morality, appropriateness requires correct procedure. The student who gets the right answer by luck does not really know: he gets no epistemic credit; his cognitive efforts cannot be classed as successful. And the same holds for morality. Here, too, someone who just happens to do the right thing by inadvertence— be it by luck or by some morally inappropriate factor like mere caprice—gets no moral credit. It is simply not enough that one does the right thing. If you borrow a saw from David with the intention of handing it over to Arnold for disposal instead of returning it to its rightful owner, you do not get off the hook of moral reprehension if you mistake Arnold for David in the darkness and inadvertently restore that implement to its rightful owner. And the same with justice. The judge who browbeats the jury into finding the defendant innocent because he "likes her looks" is not doing justice—even if she actually happens to be innocent. That defendant in our example is certainly lucky, but she is not a lucky recipient of justice, because she does not receive justice at all. Here, too, chance severs the normative chain.

With all such normative issues—justice, knowledge, morality, etc. —what matters is right results rightly arrived at; to get things right by chance—by inadvertence and pure luck—does not suffice for normative achievement. And this means that there is, in fact, no such thing as epistemic or judicial luck, because in all such cases the golden chain of appropriateness is severed by luck.

In particular, if luck alone underpins the claims your actions have to being moral, then they are, in fact, not moral at all. Morality is secure against the luck-sensitive issue of how things chance to turn out. Here luck can play no determinative role.

VIII

CAN THE TIGER BE TAMED?

"Good luck!" was Theodore Roosevelt's favorite parting expression.[1] But of course the reasonable person does not believe that wishing people good luck will somehow help them to get it. The expression displays good will and supportive fellow feeling; it is not a way of rendering aid.

The idea that luck is a somehow personified power or agency whose services can be enlisted and whose favor can be gained or lost is an ancient belief, reflected in classical antiquity by the thriving cult of the goddess Fortuna. Philosophers (especially Cicero) and theologians (especially the church fathers) have consistently inveighed against such credulity, and the diffusion of Christian belief in an all-powerful deity did eventually make some headway against a superstitious belief in luck. Nevertheless, as with other ancient superstitions, such as astrology, the practice of seeking to win her favor by paying homage to Lady Luck has never been altogether extinguished.

To be sure, our fashionable modern confidence in scientific reason has undermined this tendency to some extent. We nowadays like to think that we live in a world that has been substantially rationalized, with human affairs rendered amenable to rational control. We pride ourselves on living in an age of reason, science, and technology, where the things that affect our material and social well-being are predictable, calculable, manageable. Or so at least most of us like to think, for as the German poet Goethe puts it:

> *No one is ready to luck to extend*
>   *Thanks for all those gifts that from it we take.*
> *No! All of us much prefer to pretend*
>   *That we ourselves our own fortunes do make.*[2]
> (my trans.)

But such a congratulatory self-image is in large measure delusory. Now, as ever, human life largely proceeds in ways not of our making or choosing. Reason can, at best and at most, project its small light into the darkness of luck-determinative chance, chaos, willfullness, and unknowing that surrounds us. No matter how carefully we plot our journey, an unexpected squall can always blow us off course. Man proposes, but the disposing is, often as not, at the mercy of circumstances beyond our control. How matters actually eventuate, be it for our good or ill, is only too frequently a matter of sheer luck—prudent caution notwithstanding.

What stance shall we take toward a world of chance, where the prospect of good and bad luck dogs us at every step? Perhaps the most critical counsel is: *Be realistic*—accept luck for what it is, the offspring of impredictability. So do not try to manage and manipulate a force that will brook no domestication. After all, luck is not a power or agency of some sort. Like a harsh climate or an economic boom, luck is not a *thing* but a feature of the world's modus operandi, a conjuncture of events that comes into being when people's interests are significantly affected by fortuitous or unpredictable developments. To treat the term *luck* as a substantive, objectifying expression is to invite distorting misunderstandings. And the idea of propitiating such a potency is simply unthinking superstition, its popularity notwithstanding.

Of course, people do take innumerable measures to control and manipulate luck—witness the widespread belief that luck (be it good or bad) comes in threes and that recourse to a whole host of objects or practices supposedly brings good or bad luck. Superstition is rampant in this domain. Good luck is supposedly provided by carrying a rabbit's foot, wearing a good-luck charm, seeing one's lucky star, finding a four-leaf clover, finding a horseshoe, finding a pin, encountering lucky numbers, tripping upstairs, touching a famous person, eating herring on New Year's Day, and so on. Again, the things that supposedly bring bad luck are also legion: walking under a ladder, encountering a black cat, stepping on cracks in a sidewalk, breaking a mirror, encountering a 13 or other unlucky numbers, wishing a performer success, mentioning Macbeth to an actor, and the like. And to ward off bad luck, we cross our fingers, knock on wood, take our Christmas trees down by Epiphany. The would-be manipulation of luck is an absurd commonplace.

Proverbial counsels accordingly proliferate in this domain. When things go well, you should "thank your lucky stars." You should avoid acting on an unlucky day (Friday the 13th)[3] and be sure to wear a luck-promoting object (a good-luck charm). The traveler carries a Saint Christopher's medal, the tennis player wears his lucky shirt, the salesman sports his lucky tie. Beau Brummell haunted the gaming tables with his lucky sixpence in his pocket. Admiral George Dewey wore a rabbit's foot at the battle of Manila Bay, and when it was later exhibited in the United States, this talisman became enormously popular.[4] But, of course, all this hocus-pocus is no more than an attempt to control the uncontrollable.

Many otherwise sensible people go along with superstitious measures to control luck "just in case," on the basis of the idea that "it can't do any harm." But this idea is questionable. It all turns on the deeply problematic idea that luck is a potency that can somehow be manipulated. But this is mere foolishness. It withdraws luck from the domain to which it belongs—that of uncontrollable chance or unavoidable ignorance—and domesticates it to the more familiar and comfortable realm of the controllable. And it thereby does various sorts of harm, by diverting effort and attention from more promising safeguards, inducing less sagacious people to behave in an even more foolish manner, and encouraging the spread of superstition.

Since luck hinges on the fortuitous, there simply is no way to manipulate or control it. After all, if luck could be effectively manipulated, then it would cease to be what it by hypothesis is, namely, actual *luck*. If luck could be managed, we would not have the proverb "You can't beat a fool for luck." The gambler who "just knows" that he's going to be lucky today is riding for a fall.

It must be conceded that sometimes the superstitious feeling that "luck is on one's side" can make a difference—namely, in circumstances where one's mental attitude counts because a feeling of confidence can affect performance. When a salesman is dealing with a difficult customer or a tennis player with a tough opponent, the heartening feeling that today is one's lucky day—that on this occasion success will come one's way even "against the odds"—can make a real difference in one's prospects. Obviously, in situations where the psychic boost can engender better performance, the sentiment "I feel lucky today" can be productive. But where this is not the

175

case—as with genuine games of chance (like betting at roulette or casually playing the ponies)—it is an invitation to frustration. Luck as such doesn't take sides; if it did, it would not be what it in fact is.

To be sure, various situations are ambiguous from the standpoint of luck, involving a two-sided mixture of chance on the one hand and competent performance on the other. And in such cases, confidence—however problematically based—can indeed "improve one's chances for success." The baseball batter who steps up to the plate with an "I can do it" attitude enhances his prospects, while the one who takes the view that "this pitcher is just too good for me" is going to be in trouble. In such a confluence of skill and chance, one can foster the cause of good luck by the "power of positive thinking"—and impede it through the "power of negative thinking." And the matter means yet another aspect. The great wire walker Philippe Petit fell just once: thirty feet while practicing for the Ringling Bros. Barnum & Bailey's Circus. When he resumed his dangerous act after recovering, he pranced across a high wire for nearly half an hour to the lively music of Ravel's *Bolero*. This, he said "restored his confidence that he wouldn't fall and couldn't fall."[5] Such a stance is clearly unrealistic, once we acknowledge that chance is involved. But it is not utterly unreasonable, though, to be sure, it is a matter less of manipulating luck than of manipulating psychology. For even while recognizing that luck is not controllable, we may—as a realistic recognition of our unrealism—sometimes do well to proceed as though it were. Only through this sort of "inconsistency" may we actually be able to do our best. In the self-management of an imperfect being, a certain unreasonableness may make some sense.

One must, however, avoid the tempting but catastrophic mistake of considering luck a harnessable force or agency in nature—or a power or potency that people can manage. And it is precisely the fact that luck cannot be controlled that makes an absurdity of the unfortunate position of blaming the luckless victim and taking the unfeeling and uncomprehending line that, when people have bad luck, they have "brought it on themselves."

2. LUCK CAN BE INFLUENCED NOT BY SUPERSTITIOUS MANIPULATION BUT BY PRUDENCE

Though it lies in the nature of things that we cannot eliminate the machinations of chance and unknowing from human affairs, we can certainly come to *understand* the ramifications of this ineliminable situation better and thereby to accommodate ourselves to it more effectively. For example, we can to some extent guard against bad luck by various prudent measures—common caution, insurance, hedging one's bets—which can provide some cushioning against unfortunate eventuations. And alertness, preparedness, thoughtful timing, and the like can serve to put us into a better position to create and seize opportunities and so to help put us in the way of good luck.

The workings of luck as such are beyond our reach; whether or not we will be lucky or unlucky in particular circumstances and situations is something over which—virtually by definition—we can have no control. But the scope of what is left to luck—the extent to which we expose ourselves to the impact of chance—is something we can indeed influence. The bachelor male who moves from a job in a factory that employs only men into an office heavily staffed with unmarried women thereby obviously improves his chances of finding a wife and securing domestic bliss—or its opposite. The person who enters the competition at least creates the opportunity to win; one who does not has no chance.[6] The student who works hard does not just trust to luck to pass the examination. The traveler who maps the journey out in advance does not rely on luck to produce a helpful and knowledgeable person to show the way. Foresight, planning, sensible precaution, preparation, and hard work can all reduce the extent to which we require luck for the attainment of our objectives. To be sure, we can never eliminate the power of luck in our affairs—human life is everywhere punctuated by risks of mishap. But we certainly can act so as to enlarge or diminish the extent of our reliance on luck in pursuing our desired ends. Luck as such cannot be controlled, but in many situations its workings can be given a helping (or hindering) hand. There is everything to be said for striving to bend one's efforts into constructive lines and then—win, lose, or draw—taking rational satisfaction in the fact of having done the best one could. (Admittedly, there will be circumstances when this is pretty cold comfort—as when one finds oneself on a tumbril headed for the guillotine. But that, alas, is just life!)

What is regrettable about the superstitious management of luck —keeping track of one's unlucky days, carrying a rabbit's foot, planning by lucky numbers, and all the rest—is that it is counterproductive. It diverts time, energy, and effort away from the kind of effective planning and working that has some real chance of improving one's lot. For people can indeed come to grips with luck in some promising ways—not through those occult procedures but by thoughtful planning and sensible action. They can position themselves so as to afford good luck a chance. And, no less important, they can take sensible measures to shield themselves against the consequences of bad luck. Be it in business, romance, or warfare, one can manage one's affairs so as to reduce reliance on luck. Only the commander who maintains a strategic reserve is in a good position to take advantage of an unexpectedly created opportunity. Napoléon's well-known tendency to entrust commands to marshals whose records showed them to have "luck on their side" did not (in all probability) so much betoken superstition as a sensible inclination to favor those who had a demonstrated record for the sagacious management of risks in warfare. (On the other hand, Napoléon was not always that rational; he often characterized Josephine as his lucky talisman and later became convinced that divorcing her had caused his luck to run out and engendered his downfall.)

Chance, while in one way random, yet in another way favors the prepared—those who are so situated as to be in a position to seize opportunities.[7] We can indeed do various prudent things that facilitate good luck and safeguard against the bad. It is the competent player and the shrewd (and well-bankrolled) investor who are in the best position to take advantage of the opportunities that luck affords. Many are those for whom good luck created chances that swiftly became lost opportunities. A person who is actively on the lookout for unanticipated openings can best take full advantage of them when they occur. And one can also invite bad luck, doing imprudent things that render one more vulnerable to disaster by failing to take sensible precautions against the all-too-common prospect that things may go wrong. Where luck is concerned, there is no better counselor than prudence.

3. TAKING ONE'S CHANCES

It is part of the irony of the human situation that it is precisely the able, enterprising, venturesome, imaginative people who are also particularly at the mercy of ill luck. The reason for this lies in the reverse of the prudential principle "Nothing ventured, nothing gained"— namely, "Something ventured, something risked." After all, whenever we pursue some collaborative aim, endeavoring to achieve some putative good in circumstances where the cooperation of people or of nature is required to achieve success or avert failure, we lay ourselves open to prospective defeat at the hands of unforeseeable developments and so become vulnerable to bad luck (though, of course, to good luck as well).

Risks are not only pervasive but protean. In one sense of this term, there are as many "kinds of risks" as there are kinds of negativities in human affairs. Risks, like goods and evils, come in different types and sizes, depending on the sort of negativity or hazard that will arise "when things go wrong." A few possibilities include loss of possessions and economic assets; loss of liberty (e.g., through imprisonment); loss of privilege, opportunities, etc.; loss of face; devaluation in the esteem of others; loss of what is familiar, accustomed, accepted; illness, injury, or physical impairment; anxiety or worriment; psychological harm or impairment; death (i.e., loss of one's very existence); harm to valued persons; harm to valued causes; environmental degradation or disruption. The list goes on. Life being what it is, the possibilities of misfortune are literally limitless.

But in calculating and managing our risks, we can at least achieve a prudent minimization of the extent to which we rely on pure luck. From the moment we come into the world, we have something to lose. And for every possible kind of bad thing that can happen, there is, in principle, the prospect of acting so as to risk its happening— to increase the chance of its realization. The question in human action is never the indefinite one of whether to accept risk or not— the answer here is a foregone conclusion. The question can only be whether to accept this risk or that one. Action is always a matter of balancing one risk against another, of chancing one hazard or another. And whenever there are risks, the prospect of luck—while good and bad—comes upon the scene. In human affairs, impredictability and risk go hand in hand: the issue of prediction is pervasively interconnected with that of risk, since action in the face of impredictability inevitably involves risk—be it a risk of actual harm or merely one of things not working out as we would wish.

Some risks we assume by deliberate acts, as with the possible loss that we invite when we bet on the ponies. Other risks are essentially involuntary and simply come our way in virtue of our living when and where we do—the risks of falling victim to "acts of God," for example, or suffering harm through such acts of fortuitous violence as are inflicted by terrorists or random shooters. We are vulnerable creatures, living our lives within a sea of risks. The environment we inhabit confronts us with major risks,[8] and so does virtually every choice we make and every action we take. "Taking chances" is an ineliminable part of human existence. But in calculating our risks, we can at least achieve a prudent minimization of the extent to which we rely on pure luck.

Nevertheless, the world's realities being what they are, there are circumstances in which we would be well advised to take explicit and deliberate steps to make room for sheer luck. Consider triage situations in organ transplantation cases where a significant shortage of donor organs obtains. When the shortage is sufficiently acute, rational selection factors such as likelihood of success, expectation of future life, and the like only go so far. And when the limit of their eliminative power is reached, there is no point in pretending that specific selections are the product of impartial rationality. At this point, chance becomes our most defensible resort. After all, life itself is a chancy business, and even the most rational of human arrangements can cover this over to a very limited extent at best. By leaving a place for sheer luck in the overall operation of the triage selection system, we acknowledge the unsuitability of any merely human deliberations for the work of "playing God."

4. COMMON SENSE IN DEALING WITH MATTERS OF LUCK

What is the sensible way to come to terms with the reality of luck? What exactly should we *do* about it? We are certainly not helpless here. As the preceding deliberations indicate, there is much we can do.

Inviting good luck. To maximize one's exposure to good luck, to give luck a chance, one should capitalize on opportunities that put one in a situation where favorable developments can occur. One cannot win the race one does not enter. Only by placing ourselves in a position where luck can do us some good can we hope to realize its benefits. By buying a ticket for the lottery, we can possibly win it; by improving our qualifications, we can increase the chances of securing a good job. And, of course, if we buy two lottery tickets, we double the chance of winning. The principles of prudential risk management are clearly matters of simple common sense, and once our objectives are settled, prudence calls for keeping the odds on our side; good luck is operative to the extent that success comes our way in the face of the odds. Either way—whether assessing prudence or adjudging luck—the determination of probabilities is a crucial factor. We can in many cases determine—or at least influence—the probability of good or bad luck coming our way. When we drive twice as far, we double the chance of having an automobile accident. And while the drunk driver may not have an accident—that is, he may get away with his reckless behavior—if bad luck does come his way, it does so more or less by invitation, since through his own action he has vastly increased the chances that something could go wrong.

Playing the odds. It is almost always advisable to keep the odds on one's side by managing risks with reference to determinable probabilities—thereby also reducing the extent to which one places reliance on sheer luck. Wherever we can make a reasonable calculation of the prospects, we improve our chances. Flying in the face of the odds is by its very nature imprudent. Even when we "throw caution to the wind," we do not necessarily abandon all sensible trust in skillful effort and place our reliance on luck alone.

Avoiding undue risks. It is another cardinal rule of prudence to minimize one's exposure to bad luck: not to take undue or unnecessary chances. After all, people who do not court danger (who do not try to cross the busy roadway with closed eyes) need not count on luck to pull them through. The course of wisdom is to keep oneself out of harm's way. To avoid needless risks, one's motto should be: Do not push your luck. Do not do foolish, ill-advised, risky things and count on good luck to rescue you from difficulties. The sagacious person avoids unnecessary and excessive risks, keeping the odds in her favor so as to minimize the extent to which reliance need be placed on luck to save the day.

Buying insurance. It is another tried and true resource for impredictability management to provide some protection and buffering against the inevitable occurrences of unlucky eventuations; to build up some strategic reserves against misfortunes. People make proper provisions against unforeseeable difficulties by way of insurance, hedging, and the like. In effect, this involves forming a multiparticipatory syndicate, where the many who do not lose out by the realization of an impredictable outcome cover the losses of those few who do, paying this price in advance to secure a similar benefit for themselves should matters eventuate in their being the losers. While insurance does not alter the impredictability of the outcome (one's house catching fire, one's ship foundering in a storm), it alters the situation so as to modify and offset the loss that would ensue. The process of hedging one's bets—for example, by buying futures, i.e., options for funds or for goods for future delivery—is closely analogous to this. All such strategies are ways of coming to terms with impredictability and not ways of overcoming it. They provide the means for making the best of things in a predictively difficult world.

Extending one's knowledge. Clearly, the most promising way of handling impreditability due to ignorance rather than to chance is to pursue further inquiries to eliminate or reduce the ignorance at issue and to develop the information needed to arrive at rational decisions instead of "trusting to luck." To be sure, the limited opportunities of the conditions of the place and time—and the costs and delays involved—mean that we cannot always achieve as much as we would like. But doing what we can in this direction is generally worthwhile.

There is another way of diminishing the role of luck in life—the rather radical remedy of the ancient Stoics and Epicureans. They recommended an indifference (*apathê*) that diminishes the realm of things in which we take interest. And this, of course, takes luck out of it. (After all, luck can play no role where no benefits or negativities are at stake.) But this particular remedy comes at too high a cost.

5. MORE ON HANDLING RISKS

Unfortunately, people often proceed in such ways that even good luck does them no good. The gambling addict who insists on playing his winnings away is reasonably unable to profit by them, no matter how well luck favors him. No matter how well luck and talent may serve a Napoléon in producing a long string of victories, it does no good for one who persists in prolonging the series of battles to the point of eventual defeat. To be "hungry"—to look out for opportunities to improve one's condition and be prepared to seize them—is a good thing; but to be "greedy"—to run all sorts of risks and count on luck to come to one's aid—is eminently unwise.

To be sure, people of persistence and determination can often overcome bad luck. Meeting life's upsets with an energetic and positive response, they treat bad luck as a challenge to the achievement of greater goods. George Washington lost New York and had a hard winter at Valley Forge, but with tenacious persistence he won through at the end. Lord Cornwallis may have suffered humiliation at Yorktown, but he managed to pick up the pieces and go on to a splendid career in India.

185

In risk curtailment, as in all product-control, *quality-monitoring* situations, a characteristic relationship obtains. If we tighten the net too much, too little gets through; if we loosen it up, then too much gets through. In all risk-involving situations, two sorts of errors are possible: overreliance on good luck ("pushing one's luck," counting on luck to bail one out), or underreliance on luck ("distrusting one's luck," seeing oneself as foredoomed to have bad luck). These errors result in overly daring or overly cautious comportment, with the obvious unfortunate consequences of failures incurred or opportunities lost. In seeking to eliminate type 1 errors (errors of commission—failures and malfunctions), we inevitably produce type 2 errors (errors of omission—missed opportunities). And the converse holds as well. Both kinds of errors accordingly betoken a counterproductive unrealism. In our seeking a risk-free life, we may well create an intolerable situation. The sensible thing is to have a policy that strikes a proper balance between malfunction and missed opportunities—a balance whose "propriety" must be geared to a *realistic* appraisal of the hazards and opportunities at issue. Man is a creature condemned to live in a twilight zone of risk and opportunity.

The cardinal rule is: *Act prudently*. Do what you reasonably can to enhance the opportunities for good luck and to diminish the prospects for bad. All the usual principles of sensible care come into operation here: Avoid needless risks. Don't push your luck. Don't run risks out of all proportion to the potential benefits and count on luck to save the day for you. And—contrariwise—don't refrain from taking properly calculated risks. Don't refrain from doing sensible things that can put you in luck's way.

Of course, encompassed within the injunction to act prudently is the instruction: *Act!* Virtually any human enterprise is subject to the risk of failure, mishap, or disappointment. Nevertheless, the old precept holds true: "Faint heart ne'er won fair lady." One must resist the call of laziness or the fear of failure.

The bottom line is that while we cannot *control* luck through superstitious interventions, we can indeed *influence* luck through the less dramatic but infinitely more efficacious principles of prudence. In particular, three resources came to the fore here:

Risk management: managing the direction of and the extent of exposure to risks, and adjusting our risk-taking behavior in a sensible way over the overcautious-to-heedless spectrum.

Damage control: protecting ourselves against the ravages of bad luck by prudential measures, such as insurance, "hedging one's bets," and the like.

Opportunity capitalization: avoiding excessive caution by positioning oneself to take advantage of opportunities so as to enlarge the prospect of converting promising possibilities into actual benefits.

Yet the unhappy fact remains that all the planning in the world will take us only so far. For it lies in the nature of things that the best-laid plans of imperfect creatures will frequently misfire. We obviously want to bring the best achievable possibilities to realization, and to this end will—where rational—deploy such resources as rational inquiry, planning and preparation, risk management, and the like. But the extent to which such useful coping strategies actually enable us to shape and influence (let alone control) our future is— all too clearly—limited. There is only so far we can go in managing the role of luck in our lives. In the face of our cognitive and practical limitations, the best we can in general achieve is to diminish the scope of unexpected developments and provide safeguards against the negative consequences we cannot avert.

We live in a world of chance and chaos, choice and contingency —a world in which rational foresight can go only so far. We can certainly manage our affairs prudently so as to render the future *somewhat* less precarious. But, life being what it is, our effectiveness in this direction is bound to be far less than we would ideally like. "Probability is the guide of life," said Bishop Joseph Butler. In general, even when we do all we can to play the odds clearly, we can act only on imperfect estimates. And in matters where we have insufficient, let alone incorrect, information—as we so often do—we take a "leap in the dark." Insofar as unavoidable ignorance regarding the future is an inescapable feature of human life, luck (both good and bad) is an inevitable reality that has to be accepted as such.

IX

LIFE IN A HALFWAY HOUSE

1. THERE'S NO TAKING THE LUCK OUT OF LIFE

From the very beginning of the species, much human effort has been devoted to devising practices, systems, and institutions to make the future more tractable by reducing the scope of chance and impredictability in our affairs. Our early shift from hunter-gatherer to farmer, from nomad to settler, was clearly designed to make it possible to meet our needs and achieve our ends with greater assurance. And, over the millennia, an immense amount of human ingenuity and toil has been expended in this direction of diminishing the role of luck in life.

In particular, the issue of "control over nature" lies at the core of the scientific enterprise. But one cannot avoid recognizing that this has far more complexity than appears on first view. For just exactly how is this business of control to be understood? Clearly, control consists in bending the course of events to our will, of attaining our ends within nature. But this involvement of "our ends" brings to the fore the problematic issue of our own contribution. After all, if we are inordinately modest in our demands (or very unimaginative), we may even achieve "complete control over nature," in the sense of being in a position to accomplish *whatever we want to do,* yet attain this happy condition in a way that betokens very little real capability. The fact is that the project of achieving the practical mastery of "doing whatever we want" can never be perfected in a satisfactory way. For this clearly hinges on what we want, and what we want is shaped by what we think possible, and this is accordingly something that hinges crucially on theory—on our (unavoidably imperfect) beliefs about how things work in this world. We can never safely move from apparent to real adequacy in this regard; we cannot adequately ensure that seeming perfection is more than just that. The very idea of perfecting "control over nature" is something deeply problematic.[1]

Moreover, we have to recognize that our power to shape the course of events is small—that our prospects of control are severely limited. One such factor is *causal impotence*. There is simply nothing that most of us can do (unlike, say, the Secretary of the Treasury or the chairman of the Federal Reserve Bank) to influence the stock market: the issue is one that lies beyond the reach of our powers. Another limiting factor is *inadequate information*—and predictive information in particular. If I knew which stocks would rise tomorrow, I would make money—buying some of them is within my power—but, of course, I lack any such knowledge. For us humans, the future is veiled, as it were, in a cloud of unknowing; very little can be seen at a distance—and that little without clarity. But as things draw near, the fog of unforeseeability dissipates and we can—frequently—make out its features with greater, but still imperfect, detail. And a future we cannot foresee is, for this reason, a future we cannot control. Historical experience and theoretical analysis alike indicate that both these factors, powerlessness and ignorance, severely limit our capacity to manipulate nature's course of events and to control the future consequences of our present endeavors.

And here, of course, lies the root of luck. For it is clear that where we cannot achieve knowledge and cannot exercise control we are bound to be at the mercy of luck. Given the limits of human knowl-

edge and power, and given the prominence on the world's stage of
the contingency-engendering factors of chance, chaos, and choice—
to say nothing of ignorance as such—luck is something that we simply have to accept as an inevitable fact of life.

It is questionable if even good luck is an unalloyed good. Super-
ficially it seems that it must be so. Certainly, any sensible person
would rather be lucky than unlucky. But the matter is not so straightforward. There are, after all, two ways of being lucky: to have unexpected good things happen and to have expected bad things not
happen. A life that is a series of narrow escapes and fortuitously
evaded mishaps is lucky all right, but it is not an enviable one. Some
strokes of luck we would just as soon do without. Better a life that
is dull and uneventful than one that is made tolerable only through
the good luck of a long chain of barely averted disasters. And consider
the challenge of the old riddle "Is it better to be lucky than smart?"
The answer, of course, is that it very much depends. It may seem
more advantageous to *have been* lucky than to have been smart, because then the money is already there and "A bird in hand is worth
two in the bush." But there's the other side of it, that luck without
smarts isn't much good, because, as the saying has it, "A fool and
his money are soon parted."

The profound importance of luck thus roots in its being one of
the salient features of the human condition. There simply is no way
to take the luck out of a life whose future we can neither control nor
foresee. Luck is a fundamental and inevitable aspect of human finitude reflecting our vulnerability in a world over which we have imperfect cognitive and practical mastery. To be sure, fate and fortune
treat some of us more kindly than others. But even they afford no
absolute security. No one stands on ground so secure that it is simply

impossible for an abyss to open up at his feet. The chance of a disaster of some sort is ever present. We can never dispense totally with luck.

2. LIFE IN A HALFWAY HOUSE

Given that we cannot possibly eliminate the role of luck in life, the question remains: Would we want to do so if we could? Is luck's role in human life an unmitigated misfortune? Would we even want the project of cognitive predictive control to be perfectible, thereby eliminating the element of chance and rendering the future "a sure thing"? A host of disturbing questions crop up at this point. How much would we actually want to know about the future—at any rate, about that relatively near-term future that is most relevant to ourselves and those we know and care about? Would we really want to have foreknowledge of the suffering that the yet unturned pages of time and circumstance hold in store for us and our children and their posterity—the catastrophes and misfortunes and suffering that await us all? These are challenging questions. And their resolution calls for some challenging acknowledgments. For, in fact, there are few punishments that could be inflicted upon a person that would be as bad as having to confront the timetable of one's future—being informed station by station, as it were, of all the major eventuations of one's life on earth. What misfortune will not be multiplied by anticipation, what triumph not diminished by foreknowledge of its certainty and its impermanence?

It is the element of openness—of uncertainty—that gives our human present its savor and endows our envisioned future with a suspenseful interest. The factors of contingency and impredictability play a central and definitive part here. There is a great experiential difference between the original game and the replay, where the outcome is already a "foregone conclusion." Sheer contingent impredictability gives life's eventuations a special interest. It is the aspect of uncertainty within strictly defined limits that makes such genres as the detective story or the horror movie psychologically effective and successful. In general, the unsurprising is, for that very reason, uninteresting. (No one finds yesterday's news all that intriguing.) We admire the technical skill of the sword swallower. But the ever-present chance that something may possibly go wrong adds a special thrill to the process. A pastiche of foregone conclusions makes life dull, uninteresting, insupportable. No one wants to watch a match between a top team and the neighborhood amateurs. Nobody wants to watch the same sporting event for fifty television replays. It is the unexpectedness and impredictability of a contest between two evenly matched teams that lends interest to a sporting event.

Erich Fromm put his finger on the nub of the matter. "Man is the only animal that can be *bored*, that can be discontented, that can feel a need to be evicted from paradise. Man is the only animal for whom his own existence is a problem which he tries to solve and from which he cannot escape. He cannot go back to the prehuman state of harmony with nature."[2] Chance, novelty, surprise, and unpredictability—in sum, luck—are factors which serve to make human existence a viable proposition. Our psychological and emotional condition is such that we would not want to live in a preprogrammed world—a world where the rest of our fate and future is preordained and indeed prediscernible in the realities of the present. Even at the price of falling victim to chance and haphazard, we yearn for novelty and innovation—for a liberation from an inevitability programmed by the settled determinations of the past. The human yearning for new experiences, prospects, and possibilities is surely characteristic of what makes us the sorts of creatures we are. For we who see even a "predictable" novel or play in a decidedly negative light, an unfailingly "predictable" life would be a disaster. To eliminate luck, we would have to lead totally routinized lives. Like a colony of insects or a species of fish, we would seek out and eventually adjust to virtually stable conditions. But this is just not our style. (Had we been content with static predictability, we could have remained in the Garden of Eden.) Homo sapiens is a creature of innovation endowed with an insatiable need to explore, to discover, to find novelty.

A degree of uncertainty is an important "spice of life"—although, as with other spices, too much of it is undoubtedly a bad thing. However, the element of psychological distance is important. When our own fat is not too much in the fire—when it is not our own immediate fate that hangs in the balance—then ignorance is bliss. And when our own fate—our own security and well-being (or that of those near and dear to us)—is at risk, then impredictability is not so much a source of special interest as a ground for concern and anxiety. A Kurdish holy man in contemporary Iraq who receives predictive messages from a twelfth-century predecessor in his dreams is quoted as explaining his unwillingness to share all of them, saying, "There is a lot I do not tell to others. How much can people accept? It is often best in this world to be ignorant."[3] There is much wisdom in this stance. For is it not one of the things that make our ever-continuing transit into the future bearable—that we do not know what it will bring? The veil of ignorance leaves room for hope, and the destruction of hope is the worst of evils.

Predictability, then, is not a be-all and end-all. We humans do need order and predictability. But we also need novelty and innovation to nourish our minds and spirits. We play games of chance, seek out stories and plays with unpredictable "suspense" endings, and pursue breaks in life's workaday routine precisely to make our existence less predictable—less dull, routine, and boring. Arthur Schlesinger, Jr., has given eloquent formulation to this point:

> I suppose the human yearning for knowledge of the future is insatiable. That is why fortune tellers and astrologers and Tarot card dealers and palm readers flourish. Yet how lucky it is that the future itself consistently frustrates those who purport to unravel it. For, if the future could be predicted, what fun would remain in life? Pervasive predictability implies a deterministic universe that threatens to render human freedom an illusion. It is the very indeterminacy of things that emboldens us to believe that, within limits, we can make our own future. So let us bless history for continuing to outwit all our certitudes.[4]

Luck's great contribution is exactly this—to outwit all those comfortable certainties. The gift of total insight into our own future would be a poisoned chalice. For life as we know and want it, our own human microenvironment needs a peculiar combination of these two factors. Unless we are prepared to cease to be what we are—to abandon the Spinozistic drive to self-preservation that impels every natural species to seek to perpetuate itself as the sort of creature it is[5]—we have to accept the limited scope of predictability as a good thing.

And luck makes yet another important contribution on the human scene. It means that the race is not always to the swift—that others, too, can occasionally have a chance. Luck thus exerts a healthy democratizing influence in preventing life from being altogether a meritocracy. There is a tug of war between justice and fairness. Justice says, To each according to his deserts. Fairness says, *Everyone* deserves a chance. Life being what it is, only talented and hard-working people can get to be concert soloists, navy admirals, or corporate CEOs. But anyone can get lucky and win the lottery. Insofar as we hold fairness as a coordinate value with justice, then luck too makes an important contribution to the quality of life. It holds out rays of hope for those whose chances of actual achievement are slim.

Only with God and his angels is luck out of the picture, and angels we humans certainly are not. To eliminate luck from our lives would be to turn us into something else: paragons for whose nature we have not the capacity—and perhaps not even the desire. And the risk of bad luck is the other side of the coin with which we pay for the prospect of good luck. The ambiguity of existence in a world where luck holds sway and uncertainty plays a role is what we need to lead a life that we—constituted as we are (that is, as evolution in this world has made us)—can possibly find satisfactory.

From the larger, philosophical point of view, then, the crucial fact is that the role of luck in human affairs highlights the cognitive situation of Homo sapiens as a being of limited capabilities. Our limitations in this regard reflect our expulsion from the Garden of Eden, which puts us at the mercy of a world over which we have only imperfect information and control. And this reality—this *human* reality—has the consequence that many modes of human excellence, many human virtues, and many human satisfactions can only secure a foothold in a world where we are limited both in what we can accomplish and in what we can foreknow.

As the church fathers insisted long ago, and Pascal reemphasized, the nobility of our human condition consists in the potential we have for accomplishing great ends with limited means. To remove the element of chance from our lives—to render them predictable by removing chance and free will—would be literally to *dehumanize* us. To be a free agent is, after all, to be a being whose choices and thus whose actions and reactions are knowable only "after the fact." It is not just (as with Immanuel Kant) that *morality* as we conceive of it requires a predictability-incompatible freedom but that *humanity* does. The acceptance of luck that is consequent upon the limitations of our knowledge and power is part of the inevitable price we have to pay for existence as the sort of creatures we actually are.

As concerns luck, we are—and must be—content to live in a halfway house. Classic evolutionary theory sees biological evolution as a mixture of chance (random variation) and cunning (adoptive selection). It thus brings chance to the very heart and core of human development. But, of course, there must be predictability too, since we could not survive without it. We need and seek novelty, uncertainty, and even danger, but it remains something we want in predictable ways. (Which is why we opt for the predictability of genres such as the detective story.) To live in ways that render our circumstances substantially foreseeable—at least as regards fundamentals—is an important feature of our human strategy for survival in a complex world.

The analogy of a game is illuminating. For us, life is like a chess match played between grand masters. In one way there is predictability: we know perfectly well how they'll move their pieces—in line with the rules of chess (here, the laws of nature). But we do not have foreknowledge as to which moves they will actually make. And this aspect of the game resembles human life: there is significant uncertainty within a framework of substantial predictability.

It is clearly the essence of humanity as we know it that we live in a halfway house as regards foreseeability—a mixture of knowing and ignorance that may change in its proportions with the condition of the times but that always hovers well between the extremes. For us, constituted as we are—as we have become, if you will, under evolution's inexorable pressures—a world that is too preponderantly predictable or too preponderantly unpredictable would prove disastrous.

One can certainly imagine a creature in whose life luck has no role, a creature who takes no interest in anything, or else one whose welfare and well-being hinge entirely on foreseeable eventuations, everything that bears on its weal and woe being preordained, preprogrammed, predictable. Such a being would lead a life without suspense and surprises, a life bereft of unexpected twists and turns, where everything always runs "like clockwork," according to predesignated plan—automatically. But this creature whose life is predictable in all its substantial details would certainly be something very different from ourselves. And we would surely not want to trade places with it. For we have been configured and compounded by natural selection to a world whose modus operandi is very different. And being what we have become, we would find it horrible to live in a luckless world.

Then, too, another important contribution to luck and chance relates to their role as something of an equalizer in human affairs—as factors that prevent a hardening of the social arteries. The mobility they create for upward and downward movement is crucial in preventing stability where the socioeconomic fate of individuals is largely settled by the resources of talent and heritage that a person acquires through birth.

We need (and apparently do actually have) a balance—a world

that is predictable enough to make the conduct of life manageable and—by and large—convenient, but unpredictable enough to make room for an element of suspenseful interest. For we do also require the presence of much that is impredictable, novel, and surprising. A totally unpredictable world would be a horror even if (contrary to hypothesis) we were able to live in it. But the opposite extreme—a world that is substantially predictable—would be an equal horror. An enjoyable life, like a good story, must have a judicious mixture of uncertainty (suspense) and predictability (security).

3. LUCK AND THE HUMAN CONDITION

But the issue cuts deeper yet. We *would* not want to remove impredictability from the world stage, because doing so would distinctively impoverish our lives. But that is not the end of the matter. We *should* not even want to remove it, because doing so would abolish us as the sorts of beings we are—or, at any rate, see ourselves as being. If all the world's occurrences were predictable—our own supposedly open decisions included—then we could not see ourselves as free agents. In a predictable world, where all our future actions could be read off from the register of the Recording Angel *in advance of the fact*, there would remain no room for human free agency. We would be no more than puppets acting out a preordained script. Our supposedly free choices would be relegated to the sphere of seeming and illusion. In sum, we would be precluded from seeing ourselves as we actually do—as free agents.

And so, to expel luck from the human scheme of things would be to achieve a desideratum at far too great a cost. For to eliminate luck is to eliminate human freedom as well: to turn us into automatons of sorts. Even as moral evil is the price we must pay for the existence of moral goodness, so uncertainty-geared luck is the price we must pay for moral freedom.

To be sure, a big question looms. We think of ourselves as free agents. But are we actually so? Big though the question may be, the answer does not really matter all that decisively in the present context. For the fact is that what we *are* for present purposes consists in what we *seem* to be—what our inner nature calls on us to see ourselves as being. An irrepressible part of us requires that we think of ourselves as free agents—that we reject any temptation to see ourselves as automatons of some kind, whose own wants, wishes, desires, choices are beside the point of decision. And, of course, to think of ourselves in this way requires acknowledging a like freedom in others. We surely have no alternative but to see them as agents whose acts are, for us—and indeed for themselves also—at least somewhat chancy and not wholly predictable.

Luck therefore is, for good and ill, a factor with which we have to come to terms in this world. And in the final analysis we would not want to have it otherwise. The pivotal point is that the elimination of luck from our lives is neither feasible (so long as we humans are free agents) nor desirable (so long as we are beings who cannot thrive in a predictable, unchancy world). A creature in whose life luck has no role would be something very different from ourselves, condemned to an existence that we ourselves—constituted as we are—would find abhorrent.

4. LUCK AND REASON

Can we possibly make good, rational sense of luck? Can a world in which things go well or ill for us fortuitously and by mere chance be coherently understood? The answer is: Of course. It is the prime achievement of reason to grasp things as they actually are. And in a world in which contingency and ignorance are living realities, where chance and unforeseeability are facts of life, reason must, can, and does come to terms with this! To be sure, it lies in the nature of things that there will not and cannot be any good reason why X is lucky and Y is not. If there were, then the matter would for this very reason not be one of luck. The fortuitousness engendered by chance, ignorance, and their congeners is a fact of life. And, as such, it is something with which a faculty of reason capable of grasping things as they are can and does come to terms. Reason, in sum, is perfectly capable of understanding the ways of luck insofar as they are understandable at all—it can recognize the limits of its own dominion in a world whose imperfect rational beings cannot achieve predictive and practical mastery.

For the traditional rationalistic philosopher, the ideal would doubtless be a world where life can be lived most successfully on principles of prudence and good sense and on such principles alone—a world where the real is altogether rational. What keeps this ideal from being realizable is the intrusion of chance, of reason's enemy—the surd. But reason itself has the last laugh here. Insofar as rationality has limitations, reason itself can recognize them.

But the fact remains that reason and prudence are our best line of defense against ill luck. It is *never* sensible to proceed unintelligently; irrationality is (rationally) indefensible. One can certainly reject or neglect reason. But one cannot do so in a sensible, rationally appropriate way.

This being so, we can come to a big question: To what extent should we live our lives on principles of reason?

People often say things like: "Rationality is cold, passionless, inhumane. It stands in the way of those many life-enhancing, unreflective, spontaneous activities that have an appropriate place in a full, rewarding, happy human life." One frequently hears such claims maintained. But they are erroneous. For one must distinguish between actions and activities that are *a-rational*, which involve little or no use of reason, and those that are *irrational*, which actually go against reason. Now, reason can and does recognize as wholly proper and legitimate a whole host of useful activities in whose conduct it plays little, if any, part—socializing, diversions, recreations, and so on. And risk taking too deserves a place on the list.[6] Reason itself is altogether willing and able to give such activities its stamp of approval, recognizing their value and usefulness.

While Homo sapiens is indeed a rational being, he is not *only* a rational being. There is more to humanity than rationality. Our natural makeup is complex and many-sided—a thing of many strains and aspects. We have interests over and above those at issue in the cultivation of reason. But there is no reason whatever why we should not be able to recognize this fact. To fail to do so would simply be unintelligent—and thus contrary to the very nature of rationality. The very fact that man is the rational *animal* means that there is a good deal more to us than reason alone—and nothing prevents our rationality itself from recognizing that this is so.

Several ancient philosophers—Aristotle preeminently—insisted on the primacy of the strictly intellectual pleasures inherent in the exercise of reason. They maintained that only the purely rational intellectual activities—learning, understanding, reasoning—yield satisfactions of a sort worthy of a rational being. Only in the pleasures of the mind did they see true satisfactions. Accordingly, they suggested that only in the pleasures that are consequent upon the exercise of reason can rational creatures take appropriate satisfaction; all else is a matter of dross and delusion.

But this line of thinking is deeply problematic. Rationality does not demand that we seek satisfaction in reason alone and view the pleasures of reason as solely and uniquely genuine. Far from it! Reason can and does acknowledge the need for diversity and variation; it can and does recognize the importance of activities that call for little, if any, exercise of reason. The importance of a *balance* of varied goods within a complex "economy of values" is something which reason itself emphasizes—even though this complex must itself encompass various mundanely a-rational goods. To insist that rational satisfaction—reflective contentment—rather than mere "pleasure" is the pivot of genuine happiness does not mean that commonplace pleasures have no legitimate place in a truly happy life. There is no sound reason why rational people need be spoilsports and have to lead a totally gray, humdrum, risk-free existence. Given that we are what we are, it would not really be reasonable to want to expel luck from the world.

People can certainly succumb to overcalculation, overplanning, and an overcommitment to various uses of reason. However, the salient fact is that rationality itself countermands this. In being "too rational" one would, strictly speaking, not be rational enough. It is perfectly rational sometimes to do heedless or even madcap things in this life—to "break the monotony" and inject an element of nov-

elty and excitement into an otherwise prosaic existence. All work and
no play makes life go stale. People can sometimes take quite appropriate pleasure from "irrational" actions—climbing mountains, betting on the ponies, dipping into a freezing river—"taking chances,"
in short. To break the mold of a colorless rationalism is, within limits,
by no means unintelligent, let alone irrational. It is part and parcel
of a deeper rationality that goes beyond the superficial. After all,
rationality aims at goods as well as goals. It is clearly in a position to
appreciate the values of enjoyment as well as those of achievement
—those that make "trusting to luck" included.

To say that reason is cold, inhumane, bloodless, and indifferent
to human values is to *misconceive* rationality as purely a matter of
means to arbitrary ends, committed to the approach of "Let's get
to the goal but never mind how, with no worry about who or what
gets hurt along the way." But such a "mechanical" view of
reason, regrettably widespread though it is, is totally inappropriate.
It rests on that familiar fallacy of seeing reason as a mere instrument that is in no position to look critically at the goals toward
whose realization it is being employed. It refuses to grant reason
that which is in fact its definitive characteristic—the use of
intelligence.

Luck is an integral and ineliminable feature of human existence.
Yet it is rather like the difficult spouse of the dictum "He can't live
with her and can't live without her." We cannot make a satisfactory
life for ourselves by relying upon luck alone, and would be ill advised
indeed to count on luck to provide the things that will, in the normal
course of things, be the fruit of toil and effort. But, on the other
hand, if luck systematically abandoned us, we would be condemned

to decidedly unsatisfying lives. And precisely because reason cannot domesticate luck, it can and does acknowledge it for what it is and manages to come to terms with it.

5. AN EVOLUTIONARY PERSPECTIVE

Coming to terms with luck is something that ought to become all the easier for us when we consider that luck has made us what we are today—at any rate at the species level. George G. Simpson has very rightly stressed the many chancy twists and turns that lie along the evolutionary road, insisting that

the fossil record shows very clearly that there is no central line leading steadily, in a goal-directed way, from a protozoan to man. Instead there has been continual and extremely intricate branching, and whatever course we follow through the branches there are repeated changes both in the rate and in the direction of evolution. Man is the end of one ultimate twig. . . . Even slight changes in earlier parts of the history would have profound cumulative effects on all descendent organisms through the succeeding millions of generations. . . . The existing species would surely have been different if the start had been different, and if any stage of the histories of organisms and their environments had been different. Thus the existence of our present species depends on a very precise sequence of causative events through some two billion years or more. Man cannot be an exception to this rule. If the causal chain had been different, *homo sapiens* would not exist.[7]

The workings of evolution—be it of life or intelligence or human culture—are always the product of a great number of individually unlikely events. The unfolding of developments involves putting to nature a series of questions whose successive resolutions produce a process reminiscent of the game Twenty Questions, sweeping over a possibility-spectrum of awesomely large proportions. The result eventually reached lies along a route that traces out one particular contingent path within a possibility-space that provides for an ever-divergent fanning out of further alternatives as each step opens up room for yet more contingent eventuations. An evolutionary process is a very iffy proposition—a complex labyrinth in which a great many turns in the road must be taken aright for matters to end up as they do.

Of course we live in a world of laws rather than one of anarchy. In nature, even chance is lawful and runs in channels canalized by laws. But, nonetheless, what concrete things come into existence is something that is dictated by chance. And, specifically, the development of the genetic biological types (species) that are found in nature—our own included!—is something that pivots on the multitude of chance events that characterize the course of evolutionary history.

If things had not turned out suitably at every stage, we would not be here. The many contingencies on the long route of cosmic, galactic, solar-systemic, biochemical, biological, social, cultural, and cognitive evolution have all turned out right; the innumerable obstacles have all been surmounted. In retrospect, it all looks easy and inevitable. The innumerable possibilities of variation along the way are readily kept out of sight and out of mind. There are simply too many critical turnings along the road of cosmic and biological evolution.

The fact is that many junctures along the way are such that, had things gone only a little differently, we would not be here to tell the tale.[8]

The ancient Greek atomists' theory of possibility affords an interesting lesson in this connection. Adopting a Euclideanly infinitistic view of space, they held to a theory of innumerable worlds:

> There are innumerable worlds, which differ in size. In some worlds there is no sun and moon, in others they are larger than in our world, and in others more numerous. The intervals between the worlds are unequal; in some parts there are more worlds, in others fewer; some are increasing, some at their height, some decreasing; in some parts they are arising, in others failing. They are destroyed by collision one with another. There are some worlds devoid of living creatures or plants or any moisture.[9]

On this basis, the atomists taught that every (suitably general) possibility is realized in fact someplace or another. Confronting the question "Why do dogs not have horns: just why is the theoretical possibility that dogs be horned not actually realized?" the atomists replied that it indeed is realized, but just elsewhere—*in another region of space*. Somewhere within infinite space, there is another world just like ours in every respect save one: that its dogs have horns. That dogs lack horns is simply a parochial idiosyncrasy of the particular local world in which we interlocutors happen to find ourselves. Reality accommodates all possibilities of worlds through spatial distribution: as the atomists saw it, *all* alternative possibilities are in fact actualized in the various subworlds embraced within one spatially infinite superworld.

This theory of virtually open-ended possibilities was annihilated by the closed cosmos of the Aristotelian world-picture, which dominated European cosmological thought for almost two millennia. The breakup of the Aristotelian model in the Renaissance and its replacement by the infinitistic view of space now familiar from Newtonian physics is one of the great turning points in the intellectual tradition of the West—elegantly portrayed in Alexandre Koyré's splendidly titled book, *From the Closed World to the Infinite Universe*.[10] The Italian philosopher Giordano Bruno had a near-demonic delight in seeing the closed Aristotelian world explode into an infinite universe spread throughout endless spaces. Others were not delighted but appalled: John Donne spoke of "all cohearence lost," and Pascal was frightened by the "eternal silence of infinite spaces," of which he spoke so movingly in *Pensées*. But no one doubted that the onset of the Newtonian world-picture represented a cataclysmic event in the development of Western thought.

Strangely enough, the refinitization of the universe effected by Einstein's general relativity produced scarcely a ripple in philosophical or theological circles, despite the immense stir caused by other aspects of the Einstein revolution. (The space-time of general relativity is, after all, even more radically finitistic than the Aristotelian world-picture, which left open, at any rate, the prospect of an infinite future with respect to time.)

To be sure, it might well seem that the finitude in question is not terribly significant, because the distances and times involved in modern cosmology are so enormous. But this view is rather naïve. The difference between the finite and the infinite is as big as differences can be and has—in this present context—the most far-reaching significance. For it means that we have no alternative to supposing that a highly improbable set of eventuations is not going to be realized in very many places, and that something sufficiently improbable may well not be realized at all. The decisive *philosophical* importance of cosmic finitude lies in the fact that in a finite universe only a finite range of alternatives can be realized. A finite universe must "make up its mind" about its contents in a far more radical way than an infinite one. And that it has decided in our favor is something that deserves to be seen—by us—as an enormous piece of good luck.

TAKING LUCK'S MEASURE

The magnitude of luck pivots on the extent to which the realization of an eventuation E is significant by way of yielding fortunate or unfortunate results for someone. It is a function of the difference that E makes for the interests at stake, which we shall here represent by $\Delta(E)$. Yet to arrive at a plausible measure, we must combine this quantity with E's probability, or rather its improbability: $1-\text{pr}(E)$. (The more likely an eventuation is, the less luck has to do with it.) In effecting this complication in the most economical way possible, we arrive at the following measure of the luck involved in E's realization:

$$\lambda(E) = \Delta(E) \times [1-\text{pr}(E)] = \Delta(E) \times \text{pr}(\text{not-}E)$$

The λ measure accordingly combines—by way of simple multiplication of those two pivotal factors—the difference for good/bad and the improbability that are at issue with a lucky (or unlucky) eventuation. Whenever the quantities at issue with the (im)probability of an outcome and its differential impact on one's fortunes can themselves be measured—which is by no means always the case—the λ-measure affords a plausible way of quantifying luck.

It should be noted, in particular, that the following plausible consequences follow automatically from the perspective of this measure:

1. Rather different ways of measuring luck (λ) will potentially arise with different measures (Δ) for assessing good or bad fortune.
2. With high probability events where $pr(E) \cong 0$, we shall have $\lambda \cong \Delta$. Here luck as such recedes into the background, and the issue comes down simply to fortune.
3. With high probability events where $pr(E) \cong 1$, we will have $\lambda \cong 0$. No luck is involved with outcomes that are virtually certain. Here luck as such simply exits from the picture.
4. In general, $\lambda \leq \Delta$. One cannot be luckier (unluckier) with an eventuation than the extent to which its realization is fortunate (unfortunate).
5. Where outcomes are equally fortunate/unfortunate (where their Δ-values are equal), the luck involved in their realization correlates with their improbability (i.e., with probabilities of their nonoccurrence): the more unlikely an eventuation, the greater the luck involved in its realization.
6. Being lucky has two contraries. It is necessary to distinguish between situations where no luck is at issue and those where someone is unlucky. No luck means $\lambda = 0$, while unlucky means λ is (very) negative.

N O T E S

INTRODUCTION

1. For the historical details, see Richard Rhodes, *The Making of the Atomic Bomb* (New York: Simon & Schuster, 1988).
2. "I have but lean luck in the match" (Shakespeare, *Comedy of Errors*, III, ii, 93). And the verb *to luck (out)* means "to turn out well by chance." (We read in Caxton's *Raynar* [1481]: "When it so lucked that we toke an ox or a cowe.")
3. While some of the best philosophical dictionaries are in German, *luck* as English speakers know it simply does not exist for these reference works because they do not accord recognition to the fact that something rather special and indeed unique is at issue when happiness or misery (*Glück* or *Unglück*) occurs through sheer accident (*Zufall*).
4. Compare *felius fortunae* (Horace, *Satires*, II, ii, 49, and/or *Epistles*, II, vi, 49).
5. Compare Plato, *Republic*, 616C; *Symposium*, 195C and 197B.
6. Pliny, *Natural History*, II, 22. An informatively detailed account of Fortuna and her many cults is given in Pauli-Wissowa, *Real-Encyklopädie der Klassischen Altertumswissenschaft*, 13ten Halbband (Stuttgart, 1910), pp. 11–42.
7. A good photograph of the former is included in the article "Greek Art" in the eleventh edition of the *Encyclopaedia Britannica* (Vol. 12 [1910], plate VI, fig. 81, opposite p. 481). Various other representations are also extant. See J. D. Beazley and B. Ashmole, *Greek Sculpture and Painting* (Cambridge: Cambridge University Press, 1932), figs. 153–56. The fullest account, profusely illustrated, is Susan B. Matheson, *An Obsession with*

Fortune: Tychê in Greek and Roman Art (New Haven: Yale University Art Gallery, 1994).

8. The *cornu copiae*, or horn of plenty, was a drinking horn filled with corn and fruit, which represented the two forms of nourishment essential to people. It was used mainly by poets and artists to symbolize good fortune (Plautus, *Poenulus*, II, 3, 5; Horace, *Epistles*, I, 12, 29, and *Odes*, I, 17, 15). The fact that money is so prominent among the good things that lie in Fortuna's gift led, already in classical antiquity, to the use of the term *fortune* for a large sum of money.

9. For other coins of this character, see Seth W. Stevenson, *A Dictionary of Roman Coins* (London: Trafalgar, 1982), p. 395. See also pp. 394–96.

10. See *Roman Imperial Coinage*, ed. Harold Mattingly and Edward A. Sydenham, vol. 5, pt. 2 (London: Sprints, 1923–81; 9 vols.), p. 228 passim.

11. There were, however, also some temples to *Fortuna virilis* (the men's Fortuna). And it was a widespread custom on Venus Day (April 1) to have "ladies' day" at men's bathhouses to invite the favor of Fortuna in matters of fertility.

12. For an account of this phenomenon with many illustrations and references to the literature, see Alan H. Nelson, "Wheels of Fortune," *Journal of the Warburg and Courtauld Institutes*, vol. 43 (1980), pp. 227–33. A game of this name and nature is a popular feature on American television today.

13. On mobile wheel-of-fortune disks in medieval and Renaissance books and manuscripts, see Michael Schilling, "Rota Fortunae," in *Deutsche Literatur des späteren Mittelalters: Hamburger Colloquium 1973*, ed. Wolfgang Hams and L. P. Johnson (Berlin: Meiner Verlag, 1975), pp. 293–313 (see esp. p. 304). See also G. Lindberg, "Mobiles in Books: Volvettes, Inserts, Pyramids, Divinations, and Children's Games," *Private Library*, 3rd series, No. 2 (1979), pp. 49–82.

14. The original text is given in *Neustria pia, seu de omnibus et singulis abbatis et prioritatibus Norminiae*, ed. Arturus du Monstier (Rouen, 1663), p. 231. Cited in Nelson, "Wheels of Fortune," p. 228.

15. John Dewey, "Time and Individuality" (1940), in *Time and Its Mysteries*, ed. Harlow Shapley (New York: Collier, 1962), pp. 141–42.

16. William Mathews, *Getting On in the World: Hints of Success in Life* (Chicago: S. Griggs & Co., 1880). This old-fashioned how-to book contains many quaint illustrations on the role of luck in life.

17. C.C.F. Greville, *The Greville Diary*, ed. P. W. Wilson, vol.1 (London: Heinemann, 1927), p. 300.

I. ENIGMAS OF CHANCE

1. Theoreticians have had to struggle to make this idea precise. A conjuncture is fortuitous if it involves the concurrent realization of events that are produced by chains of causality operating independently of one another. Accordingly, the fortuitous calls not for an abrogation of causality but only for the prospect of its operation along mutually irrelevant pathways. (Compare A. A. Carnot, "Considérations sur la marche des idées et des événements dans les temps modernes," in *Oeuvres complètes*, ed. J. Mentré [Paris, 1879], vol. 1, pp. 1–15.) A random, or stochastic, event, which operates independently of any and all causality, is thereby a fortiori fortuitous.

2. "A person's dispositions engender his fortune" ("Sui cuique mores fingunt fortunam") (Cornelius Nepos, *De viris illustribus* [Atticus], II, 6).

3. Thus, "fabrum esse suae quemque fortunae" (Sallust, *De republica ordinanda*, I, 1) and "sapiens ipse fingit fortunam sibi" (Plautus, *Trinumus*, II, ii, 84).

4. "Fate leads the willing but drags the unwilling along" ("Ducunt volentem fata, nolentem trahunt") (Seneca, *Epistolae morales ad Lucilium*, 107).

5. Plautus, *Captivi*, prologue.

6. Shakespeare speaks of a "fool of fortune" in *King Lear* (IV, vi, 196), of "fools of fortune" in *Timon of Athens* (III, vi, 107), and of "Fortune's fool" in *Romeo and Juliet* (III, i, 142).

7. As the German writer Hans Pichler puts it, often "the guardian angels of those who have luck are the unlucky" ("Die Schutzengel derer, die Glück haben, sind die Verunglückten"), in *Persönlichkeit, Glück, Schicksal* (Stuttgart, 1967), p. 47. An American proverb makes the point more succinctly: "Bad luck is good luck for someone" (in A *Dictionary of American Proverbs*, ed. Wolfgang Mieder et al. [New York and Oxford: Oxford University Press, 1992], p. 392, no. 5).

8. "Non ab hominis industria et acumine iudicioque dependens, sed a causa alia occulta."

9. In handling the issue of gender equity, I have adopted a solution that is idiosyncratic but, I think, fair and reasonable. I propose to treat an otherwise undifferentiated *someone* as male but an otherwise unidentified *person* or *agent* or *individual* as female. Thus I shall write, "Someone who loses his keys is unlucky," but "A person who loses her keys is unlucky." And I shall try to employ these two sorts of locutions in roughly equal proportions. This way we can achieve fairness while nevertheless averting the barbarism of a constantly repeated his or her.

10. The luck/fate distinction goes back to classical antiquity. For the ancients distinguished between haphazard *fortuna* (which operates by accident and chance) and necessitarian *fatum* (which operates according to fixed deterministic laws).

11. A word about impredictability/unpredictability is in order here. A phenomenon is unpredictable when it is erratic: when it varies eccentrically in ways whose unruliness can perfectly well be foreseen—at least in general terms. A phenomenon is impredictable when it eludes any and all possibility of rational prediction.

12. Instead of constantly repeating the boilerplate phrase "beneficiary or maleficiary," we shall simply speak of beneficiaries, subject to the slightly paradoxical idea of negative benefits.

13. Fortuna saevo laeta negotio et/ludum insolentem ludere pertinax/transmutat incertos honores,/nunc mihi nunc alii benigna (Horace, *Odes*, III, 29).

II. FAILURES OF FORESIGHT

1. There will, however, be some complications here. If yesterday I won the raffle whose prize I will collect tomorrow, then I am of course very lucky. That development is lucky for me because it was unforeseeable at the time, though not, of course, thereafter.

2. See note 4 of Chapter 1.

3. On these issues see Ilya Prigogine, *From Being to Becoming* (New York: W. H. Freeman Co., 1980).

4. See Joseph Ford, "What Is Chaos, That We Should Be Mindful of It?," *Physics Today*, 36/4 (1983), pp. 40–47; reprinted in *The New Physics*, ed. Paul Davies (Cambridge: Cambridge University Press, 1989), pp. 348–60.

5. Ian Stewart, *Does God Play Dice: The Mathematics of Chaos* (Oxford: Basil Blackwell, 1989), p. 298.

6. Compare Ludwig Wittgenstein, *Last Writings on the Philosophy of Psychology*, vol. 2, ed. G. H. von Wright and Heikki Nyman (Oxford: Basil Blackwell, 1982), pp. 65–67, esp. sec. 923.

7. For an informative discussion, see J. R. Lucas, *Freedom of the Will* (Oxford: Basil Blackwell, 1970).

8. On these issues, see the author's "Choice Without Preference," in *Essays in Philosophical Analysis* (Pittsburgh: University of Pittsburgh Press, 1969), pp. 111–57.

9. Of course, our control over the past is nil. That Publisher's Clearing House contest "you may already have won" is thus particularly annoying because we recognize full well that this is just plain false.

10. Only when $n = 1$ do we have: $\frac{n^2 + 1}{2} = n$

11. This is so because in general: $\frac{(n + 1)^2 - n^2 - 1}{2} = n$

12. "Die philosophische Betrachtung hat keine andere Absicht, als den Zufall zu entfernen" (*Die Vernunft in der Geschichte*, ed. D. Lasson, 5th ed. [Hamburg: S. Meiner, 1955], p. 29).

13. See the author's *The Limits of Science* (Berkeley and Los Angeles: University of California Press, 1987).

III. THE DIFFERENT FACES OF LUCK

1. *A Dictionary of American Proverbs*, ed. Wolfgang Mieder et al. (New York and Oxford: Oxford University Press, 1992), p. 393, no. 4. In England, the proverb goes back to at least 1738.
2. For further details, see *The People's Almanac Book of Lists, No. 2*, ed. Irving Wallace et al. (New York: William Morrow & Co., 1980), pp. 422–23. Several other examples are presented here, including the following: "In 1919 a 30-year-old Russian electronics engineer named Vladimir K. Zworykin emigrated to the U.S. He went to work for Westinghouse Electric Company and later for RCA. Along the way, he invented a television transmission tube and a television receiver. He became known, in fact, as the father of modern television. Just after W.W. II began, Zworykin, who was in Beirut, had to stop off in London on business before returning to New York. He started to buy a ticket for an Atlantic crossing on the SS *Athenia*. 'But I had inadvertently left my tuxedo behind in Lebanon,' Zworykin remembered in an interview with author Bruce Felton, 'and rather than endure the embarrassment of being improperly dressed in the first-class dining room during the crossing, I decided to shop for dinner dress and take a later ship.' The *Athenia* left without Zworykin. Off the coast of Ireland on September 4, 1939 the *Athenia* was torpedoed by a Nazi U-boat. It went to a watery grave with a loss of 128 lives, among them 28 Americans. The 29th American was shopping in London for a new tuxedo."
3. After a particularly severe storm moved through "Tornado Alley," stretching from northern Alabama to North Carolina, in early 1994, one clean-up worker commented: "You never know why some people are hit and others are spared. It is a very hard thing to witness" (*The New York Times*, March 29, 1994, p. A8).
4. William Mathews, *Getting On in the World: Hints of Success in Life* (Chicago: S. Griggs & Co., 1880), p. 30.
5. Note also the possibilities of an intermediate position as per the locution

"He quite reasonably thought himself to be lucky—though actually he was not."

6. A counterexample is Alvirah Meehan, the protagonist of the best-selling detective stories by Mary Higgins Clark (see especially *The Lottery Winner* [New York: Simon & Schuster, 1994]). She is a cleaning lady from Flushing, New York, who struck it rich in the lottery and used her newly gained wealth to transform herself into a celebrity detective among the rich and famous. However, it will occasion no surprise that we are here dealing with a fictional character.

7. A good journalistic discussion is presented in Lois Gould's *New York Times Magazine* article, "Ticket to Trouble" (April 13, 1995, p. 40ff.). The examples cited here are drawn from this article.

8. A *Dictionary of American Proverbs*, p. 393, no. 28.

9. Regarding issues involved in measuring the magnitude of luck, see the appendix.

IV. AN INFINITY OF ACCIDENTS

1. For an illuminating discussion, see Antonino Poppi, "Fate, Fortune, Providence and Human Freedom," in *The Cambridge History of Renaissance Philosophy*, ed. C. B. Schmitt et al. (Cambridge: Cambridge University Press, 1988), pp. 641–67. (The quotation is from p. 653.)

2. The term was coined by Horace Walpole after the Persian fairy tale *The Three Princes of Serendip*.

3. Some of the issues relevant to situations of this sort are discussed in Chapter 4, "Epistemic Luck," of Richard Foley's *The Theory of Epistemic Rationality* (Cambridge, Mass.: Harvard University Press, 1987).

4. For an illuminating account of the issues and controversies involved, see Scott Gordon, *The History and Philosophy of Social Science* (London and New York: Routledge, 1991).

5. Such ideas are criticized with verve and acuity in Isaiah Berlin's lecture "Historical Inevitability," in his book of the same title (London: Oxford

University Press, 1954). Karl R. Popper's *The Poverty of Historicism* (London: Routledge & Kegan Paul, 1957) provides another important critique.

6. John Stimson, "Social Forecasting," in *Encyclopedia of Sociology*, vol. 4, ed. E. F. Borgalle and M. C. Borgalle (New York: Macmillan, 1992), pp. 1830–35 (see p. 1832).

7. Popper, *The Poverty of Historicism*, p. ix. Other relevant writings by Popper include *The Open Society and the Enemies* (London: Routledge & Kegan Paul, 1945) and "Prediction and Prophecy in the Social Sciences," in his *Conjectures and Refutations* (London: Routledge & Kegan Paul, 1963), pp. 336–46. Popper's views on science form an important part of the grounding of his position. See especially his "Indeterminism in Quantum Physics and in Classical Physics," *British Journal for the Philosophy of Science*, 2 (1950), pp. 617–33 and 673–95. For Popper, there can be no rational prediction in history—not because history is indeterministic (quantum theory, after all, is undeterministic) but because history is literally anarchic (law-lacking). As Popper sees it, every culture and every era is a law unto itself. There are therefore no survivors among putative historical laws when they are confronted with the facts.

8. Popper, *Conjectures and Refutations*, p. 339.

9. To be sure, this principle looks remarkably like one of those laws of social process whose existence Popper calls into question.

10. Popper, *The Poverty of Historicism*, p. 128. On Popper's position and references to the extensive literature, see W. J. González, "La Interpretación histórica de las ciencias sociales," *Anales de filosofía*, 2 (1984), pp. 109–37.

11. Compare Thomas Lonergan, *Method in Theology* (New York: Herder & Herder, 1972), p. 197. In its broader, evolutionary context, this idea of "replaying" history is instructively deployed in Stephen J. Gould, *Wonderful Life* (New York: W. W. Norton, 1988).

V. VISIONS OF SUGARPLUMS

1. "Good luck never lacks for friendly welcome," says one proverb, and "Good luck never comes too late," says another.
2. This point is elaborated upon in Michael Gelven, *Why Me?* (De Kalb: Northwestern Illinois University Press, 1991), pp. 34–35.
3. William Mathews, *Getting On in the World: Hints of Success in Life* (Chicago: S. Griggs & Co., 1880). Recall the proverb "Good luck is the lazy man's explanation of another's success" (*A Dictionary of American Proverbs*, ed. Wolfgang Mieder et al. [New York and Oxford: Oxford University Press, 1992], p. 392, no. 11).
4. The proverb "Good luck is the failure's explanation of another's success" is, alas, all too true, as is its mirror image, "Bad luck is the incompetent's explanation of his own failure." This proverb has many variations, for example, "Bad luck is bad management." See *A Dictionary of American Proverbs*, p. 392, nos. 4 and 11.
5. The ensuing discussion draws upon *A Dictionary of American Proverbs*, pp. 292–93.

VI. THE PHILOSOPHERS OF GAMBLING

1. In the United States, gambling ranks high among the biggest forms of entertainment. More Americans went to casinos in 1993 than to major-league baseball games. And legal gambling revenues exceeded $30 billion, which exceeds the combined yield of movies, books, recorded music, and amusement parks and arcades. Thirty-seven states have lotteries and twenty-three have licensed casinos (data from an article by Gerri Hershey in *The New York Times*, July 17, 1994). With the rampant spread of gaming on Indian reservations and riverboats, it is estimated that by the end of the decade virtually all Americans will live within a four-hour drive of a casino.
2. Ian Hacking, *The Emergence of Probability* (Cambridge: Cambridge University Press, 1975), p. 1.

3. On Gataker, see the article in the *Dictionary of National Biography* (London: Smith, Elder & Co., 1886), vol. 7, pp. 939–40. See also *Encyclopaedia Britannica*, 11th ed. (London, 1910–11), vol. 11, p. 527. The posthumous *Adversaria miscellanea* (London, 1659), edited by his son Charles, was prefaced by his autobiography (in Latin). A helpful discussion of some of Gataker's views is given in Jon Elster, "Taming Chance: Randomization in Individual and Social Decisions," in *The Tanner Lectures on Human Values*, vol. 9, ed. G. B. Peterson (Salt Lake City: University of Utah Press, 1988), pp. 105–79.

4. *Encyclopaedia Britannica*, 11th ed., vol. 11, p. 527.

5. London: Edward Griffin, 1619; 2nd ed., cited here, published in 1627. In writing this tract, Gataker seems to have been motivated by opposition to the treatise of James Balmford (b. 1556), *A Short and Plain Dialogue concerning the unlawfulness of Playing at Cards, or Tables, or any other Game consisting in Chance* (London: R. Boile, 1593). Balmford was moved to an eventual reply to Gataker in his tract, *A Modest Reply to certain Answers which Mr. Gataker . . . in his treatise . . . gave to Arguments in A Dialogue concerning the Unlawfulness of Playing at Cards, or Tables, or any other Game consisting in Chance* (London: G. Taylor, 1623).

6. Quoted in John Ashton, *The History of Gambling in England* (London: Macmillan, 1898; rpt. Montclair, N.J.: Patterson Smith, 1969), pp. 224–25. Queen Elizabeth authorized the first English lottery in 1569. Licenses for lotteries were granted for improving the supply of water to London in 1629 and 1631. The great lottery of 1694 raised over a million pounds sterling—an incredible sum at contemporary valuation. On the Continent, lotteries had already been popular for a century, especially in the Netherlands. See Simon Schama, *The Embarrassment of Riches* (New York: Knopf, 1987), pp. 306–11, or, for a fuller account, G. A. Fokker, *Geschidenis der Loterijen en Nederland* (Amsterdam: F. Muller, 1862). The use of lotteries for charitable and public purposes is a long-

standing practice. The British Museum was established with money from a lottery.

7. Acts, 1:23–26.

8. Matthew, 27:35; Mark, 15:24; Luke, 23:34; John, 19:23–24.

9. In this way, lots were used not to play with God's plan for the world but to discern it, with the recourse to chance seen not as toying with facts but as addressing a question to its governor. This "sortilege" had long been condemned by Catholic theologians as a relic of paganism, but it was difficult to eradicate. It long continued among Protestants— Wesleyans in particular. John Wesley himself sought guidance in this way as to whether or not he should marry, as is recorded in his journal for March 4, 1737: "Having both of us [Mr. Delamotte and himself] sought God by deep consideration, fasting and prayer, in the afternoon we conferred together but could not come to any decision. We both apprehended Mr. Ingham's objection to be the strongest, the doubt whether she was what she appeared. But this doubt was too hard for us to solve. At length we agreed to appeal to the Searcher of Hearts. I accordingly made three lots. In one was writ, 'Marry': in the second 'Think not of it the year.' After we had prayed to God to 'give a perfect lot,' Mr. Delamotte drew the third, in which were the words 'Think of it no more.' Instead of the agony I had reason to expect I was enabled to say cheerfully 'Thy will be done.' We cast lots again to know whether I ought to converse with her any more, and the direction I received from God was 'Only in the presence of Mr. Delamotte' " (quoted from F. M. David, *Games, Gods and Gambling* [London: Macmillan, 1953], p. 14).

10. Augustine, *Epistola ad Honor*, 180.

11. See the reference cited in note 2 above.

12. Proverbs, 18:18.

13. See *The New York Times*, front-page report of August 25, 1959. On decisionmaking by lottery generally, see Jon Elster, "Taming Chance: Randomization in Industrial and Social Decisions," in *The Tanner Lectures on Human Values*, vol. 9, pp. 105–80.

14. "Haruspicina, quam ego rei publicae causa communisque religionis colendam censeo" (*De divinatione*, II, xii, 28). And again, "retinetur autem et ad opinionem vulgi et ad magnas utilitates rei publicae mos, religio, disciplina, ius, auqurium collegi auctoritas" (II, xxxiii, 70).

15. Compare "The Metaphysics of Gambling," chap. 6 in Franz Rosenthal, *Gambling in Islam* (Leiden: Brill, 1975).

16. For a brief account of Gracián, see the article by Neil McInnes in *The Encyclopedia of Philosophy*, vol. 3 (New York: Macmillan, 1967), pp. 375–76. For a fuller treatment, see Alan Bell, *Baltasar Gracián* (Oxford: Oxford University Press, 1921).

17. *The Economist*, August 29, 1987, p. 49. At present, the largest lottery is El Gordo ("the fat one"), held in Spain, with a prize well in excess of $100 million. In 1988, Spain's 38 million inhabitants gambled away more than $25 billion—over $650 per capita (*The New York Times*, May 14, 1989). However, even in a northern European country like Germany, more than $250 per capita is nowadays spent annually in officially sponsored games of chance (lotteries, etc.). German women are less given to gambling than men. And while low-income earners bet less than high-income ones, they do not bet any less often. Interestingly, the unemployed bet more often than other income groups. Data from *Deutschland Nachrichten* (German Information Center, New York), April 1994, p. 5.

18. For Pascal's role in the origination of the mathematical theory of probability, see Hacking, *The Emergence of Probability*, pp. 57–72.

19. *Pensées*, ed. Léon Brunschvicg (Paris: Hachette, 1914), no. 98.

20. H. F. Stewart, "Blaise Pascal," *Proceedings of the British Academy*, vol. 28 (1942), pp. 196–215 (see p. 204).

21. Quoted from John Warrington's translation of *Pensées* (London: Dent, 1960); sec. 233 in Brunschvicg edition. For further details regarding the wager argument, see also the author's *Pascal's Wager* (Notre Dame: University of Notre Dame Press, 1985).

22. *Pensées*, ed. Brunschvicg, no. 234.

23. "Trois Discours sur la condition des grands," in *Oeuvres complètes*, ed. Louis LaFuma (Paris: Editions du Seuil, 1963), p. 366.
24. Throughout the Western philosophical tradition, chance (*tuchê, casus, Zufall*) has been *defined* as an accidental concurrence of independent eventuations, which, as such, are inherently unpredictable and exempt from any mode of lawful regularity.
25. "Principles of Nature and of Grace," sec. 7, in *G. W. Leibniz: Philosophical Papers and Letters*, ed. L. E. Loemker, 2nd ed. (Dordrecht: D. Reidel, 1969), p. 639.
26. G. W. Leibniz, "Abridgment of the Controversy Reduced to Formal Arguments," in *Theodicy*, trans. E. M. Huggard (New Haven: Yale University Press, 1952), pp. 387–88.
27. Loemker, *G. W. Leibniz*, p. 687.
28. Leibniz, *Theodicy*, p. 320.
29. As J. M. Keynes noted (in *A Treatise on Probability* [London: Macmillan, 1921], p. 311n), the concept of mathematical expectation was first clearly articulated in Leibniz's 1678 essay *De incerti aestimatione* (Couturat, *Opuscules et fragments inédits de Leibniz* [Paris: F. Alcan, 1903], pp. 569–71). But here Leibniz followed the precedent of Pascal. The measurement of probability as a ratio of "equally possible" cases (i.e., the Laplacean *principle of indifference*) was his invention (*De incerti aestimatione*). For a discussion of Leibniz's work on probability, see also Hacking, *The Emergence of Probability*, chaps. 14 and 15, and passim.
30. On the effusion of gambling that accompanied the decline of morals or the time of plague in the fourteenth century, see Barbara W. Tuchman, *A Distant Mirror: The Calamitous Fourteenth Century* (New York: Ballantine Books, 1978), pp. 117, 449, 485, and passim.
31. Adapted from Marceli Defourneaux, *Spanien im goldenen Zeitalter* (Stuttgart: Reklam, 1986), pp. 239–40. For Contreras, see A. Morel-Fatio, "Soldats espagnols du 17e siècle: Alonso de Contreras," *Bulletin hispanique*, vol. 3 (1911), pp. 135–58. His biography was first published in the *Boletín de la Real Academia de Historia*, vol. 37 (1900), pp. 129–

270. The preceding generation affords the interesting example of the conquistador Mancio Serra, who died in 1589 as the last survivor of Pizarro's conquest of the Incas. He was "famous throughout Peru for having been awarded the celebrated golden image of the sun which had been the chief ornament of the Temple of the Sun at Cuzco, and was even more famous for having promptly lost it in a card game" (Lewis Hanke, *The Spanish Struggle for Justice in the Conquest of America* [Philadelphia: University of Pennsylvania Press, 1949], p. 172).

32. Compare Defourneaux, *Spanien im goldenen Zeitalter*, p. 240. Regulations and orders of all sorts pervade the military scene of the day—to little practical efforts, as their very proliferation attests.

33. In the Netherlands, gambling was intimately connected with the rise of capitalism. Speaking of the Amsterdam bourse, built in 1608, Simon Schama reports: "Like so much else in Amsterdam, both its architecture and its commercial practices were transplanted from Antwerp. The Flemish city in its day had been famous for its addiction to gambling, and in this too, its Dutch stepdaughter followed suit. Wagers were made on every conceivable opportunity, from the outcome of a siege to the sex of an impending baby. They were made on the street, in taverns, at home, in barges. . . . The line between casual betting and organized trading in stock was often blurred" (in *The Embarrassment of Riches*, p. 347). The gambling mania of the earlier part of the century set the stage for the great bursts of speculative fever that were to follow: the tulip mania, the Mississippi Scheme, and South Sea Bubble. In modern times, socialist and communist regimes not favorable to capitalism have often tried to suppress gambling, usually without success.

34. "Gaming and Wagering," *Encyclopaedia Britannica*, 11th ed., vol 11, pp. 446–450.

35. *The Diary of Samuel Pepys*, ed. R. Latham and W. Matthews, vol. 9 (Berkeley and Los Angeles: University of California Press, 1976), entry for January 1, 1668. On the role of the groom-porter, whose control over gambling goes back to Elizabethan times, see Frank Aydelotte, *Eliza-*

bethan Rogues and Vagabonds, Oxford Historical and Literary Studies, vol. 1 (Oxford: Clarendon Press, 1913).

36. Quoted from C. W. Heckthorn, *The Gambling World* (London: Hutchinson, 1898), pp. 62–63. But gaming was by no means the exclusive prerogative of high society. The sale of lottery tickets drew in all sorts: "One stream of *Coachmen, Footmen, Prentice Boys, and Servant Wenches* flowing one way, with wonderful hopes of getting an estate for three pence. *Knights, Esquires, Gentlemen and Traders, Marry'd Ladies, Virgin Madams, Jilts,* etc.; moving on *Foot,* in *Sedans, Chariots,* and *Coaches* another way; with a pleasing Expectancy of getting Six Hundred a Year for a Crown" (quoted in Lorrain Daston, *Classical Probability in the Enlightenment* [Princeton: Princeton University Press, 1988], p. 160).

37. For example, medieval Arabic scholars nibbled around the fringes of the issue in their treatment of the problem of legacies. Cf. Solomon Gandz, "The Algebra of Inheritance," *Osiris,* vol. 5 (1938), pp. 319–91. And medieval Jewish scholars addressed the question of whether meat found in the streets with x butcher shops, only y of which were kosher, could be regarded as kosher. Many such problems are canvassed in Nachum L. Rabinovitch, *Probabilities and Statistical Inference in Ancient and Medieval Jewish Literature* (Toronto: University of Toronto Press, 1973), whose treatment of the matter rightly indicates that yet another, very different route to a calculus of probability was, in principle, available.

38. This chapter draws some materials from an essay of the same title initially published in the author's *Baffling Phenomena* (Totowa, N.J.: Rowman and Littlefield, 1991).

VII. THE MUSINGS OF MORALISTS

1. There are echoes of this in the drawing of lots to select the successor to Judas as twelfth apostle. And we find vestiges of this in tie-breaking situations in various political contexts. In Sweden, chance is an arbiter prescribed by law for breaking tie votes in Parliament.

2. The question is only rarely considered. One exception is Richard A. Epstein, "Luck," *Social Philosophy and Policy*, vol. 6 (1988), pp. 17–38.

3. John Rawls, *A Theory of Justice* (Cambridge, Mass.: Harvard University Press, 1971), p. 100.

4. *A Dictionary of American Proverbs*, ed. Wolfgang Mieder et al. (New York and Oxford: Oxford University Press, 1992), p. 392, nos. 1 and 9.

5. Italian proverb encountered as early as 1642.

6. This is an issue that has been examined extensively by philosophers in recent years. An anthology of representative discussions is *Moral Luck*, ed. Daniel Stadman (Albany, N.Y.: State University of New York Press, 1993).

7. Thomas Nagel, "Moral Luck," in his *Mortal Questions* (Cambridge, Mass.: Harvard University Press, 1979), p. 25.

8. Nagel, "Moral Luck," p. 27.

9. To be sure, the law—for very good reasons—deals only with realizations; the merely would-be lawbreaker lies beyond its condemnation. But morality and law differ in this as in other regards. To fail to acknowledge this difference is in fact to take an overly legalistic view of morality.

10. The ideas at work in this paragraph are developed more fully in the author's *Philosophical Standardism* (Pittsburgh: University of Pittsburgh Press, 1994).

11. In this regard, morality differs decisively from law, which—on grounds of public policy—puts the emphasis on results and substitutes legality as such for moral rightness.

12. Nagel, "Moral Luck," p. 25.

13. "Even if it should happen that, by a particular unfortunate fate or by the niggardly provision of a stepmotherly nature, this [good] will should be wholly lacking in power to accomplish its purpose, and if even the greatest effort should not avail it to achieve anything of its end, and there remained only the good will (not as a mere wish but as the summoning of all the means in our power), it would sparkle like a jewel in its own right, as something that had its full worth in itself" (Immanuel

Kant, *Foundations of the Metaphysics of Morals*, trans. Lewis White Beck, The Library of Liberal Arts [New York: Bobbs Merrill, 1955], sec. 1, para. 3).

14. To say this is not, of course, to say that we may not want to differentiate such situations on *nonmoral* grounds—e.g., to reward only *successful* rescues or to punish only *realized* transgressions as a matter of social policy *pour encourager les autres*. Compare also Bernard Williams's example of the person who abandons a life of service to others in order to pursue his art—a decision whose moral justification (according to Williams) will ultimately hinge on how good an artist he turns out to be, which largely depends not on effort but on talent and creative vision, issues at the mercy of nature's allocation, over which he has no control (*Moral Luck*, p. 24ff.). But what earthly reason is there for seeing the *moral* situation of the talented Gauguin as being in this regard different from that of the incompetent Ignatz Birnenkopf and for excusing the former where we would condemn the latter? The impropriety of an abandonment of a moral obligation is not negated by the successes it facilitates on other fronts. Kant's point that the talented and the untalented, the lucky and the unlucky should stand equal before the tribunal of morality is well taken, and Hegel's idea that great men stand above and outside the standards of morality has little plausibility from "the moral point of view."

15. The Greek perspective is examined in Martha Nussbaum, *The Fragility of Goodness* (Cambridge: Cambridge University Press, 1986).

16. Barbara W. Tuchman, *A Distant Mirror: The Calamitous Fourteenth Century* (New York: Ballantine Books, 1978), p. 103.

17. Ibid.

18. Regarding the "survivor syndrome," see *Massive Psychic Trauma*, ed. H. Krystal (New York: Random House, 1968). For a good specimen of the psychological literature on the topic, see Bruce I. Goderez, "The Survivor Syndrome: Massive Psychic Trauma and Post-Traumatic Stress Disorder," *Bulletin of the Mayo Clinic*, vol. 51 (1987), pp. 96–113.

VIII. CAN THE TIGER BE TAMED?

1. Theodore Roosevelt was keenly attuned to his own luck. "I have played it with bull luck this summer," he wrote to Cecil Sprig Rice in 1899. "First to get into the war [as colonel of the Rough Riders]; then to get out of it [alive]; then to get elected [as governor of New York State. . . ."
(And all this even before being kicked upstairs into the vice presidency by the political boss Thomas Platt, and then succeeding to the presidency in the wake of William McKinley's assassination!)

2. Kein Mensch will bloss dem Glück was danken / Und ob's ihm Alles auch beschied / Nein, jeder hegt gern den Gedanken / Ich selbst war meines Glückes Schmied (*Fliegende Gedanken*).

3. "El martes ni te cases ni te embarques" (Neither marry nor journey on a Tuesday) runs a Spanish proverb.

4. See Adelbert M. Dewey, *The Life and Letters of Admiral Dewey* (New York: Woolfall Publishing Co., 1899), p. 499.

5. Quoted in Ralph Keyes, *Chancing It: Why We Take Risks* (Boston and Toronto: Little, Brown & Co., 1985).

6. Recall the old joke about the man who prayed nightly for the boon of winning the lottery, only to have his prayers at last elicit the booming reply from on high: "For heaven's sake, go buy a ticket."

7. When the New York Mets won the 1969 World Series despite being generally viewed as the inferior team, some attributed this outcome to "mere luck." As reported by Arthur Daley in *The New York Times*, Branch Rickey rejected this imputation with the sage observation that "luck is the residue of design" (*Sports of the Times: The Arthur Daley Years*, ed. James Tuite [New York: Quadrangle/The New York Times Book Company, 1975], p. 185; I owe this reference to Tamara Horowitz).

8. For graphic substantiation of this, see *Natural Hazards*, ed. Gilbert F. White (New York: Oxford University Press, 1974); Ian Burton et al., *The Environment as Hazard* (New York: Oxford University Press, 1978); Eric Ashby, *Reconciling Man with the Environment* (Stanford: Stanford Uni-

versity Press, 1978); and R. W. Kates, *Risk Assessment of Environment Hazard* (New York: John Wiley & Sons, 1978).

IX. LIFE IN A HALFWAY HOUSE

1. On these issues, see the author's *The Limits of Science* (Berkeley, London, and Los Angeles: University of California Press, 1984).
2. Erich Fromm, *Man for Himself: An Inquiry into the Psychology of Ethics* (New York: Holt, Rinehart, and Winston, 1947), p. 40.
3. *The New York Times*, May 31, 1993, p. 2.
4. Arthur Schlesinger, Jr., "The Future Outwits Us Again," *The Wall Street Journal*, op-ed page, September 20, 1993.
5. On the *conatus se preservandi*, see Benedict de Spinoza, *Ethics*, pt. III, prop. VIff.
6. For some interesting variations on this theme, see Ralph Keyes, *Chancing It: Why We Take Risks* (Boston and Toronto: Little, Brown & Co., 1985).
7. George Gaylord Simpson, "The Nonprevalence of Humanoids," *Science*, 143 (1964), pp. 769–75; also in *This View of Life: The World of an Evolutionist* (New York, 1964), pp. 57–73.
8. These evolutionary considerations are elaborated upon in "Extraterrestrial Science," in the author's *The Limits of Science*.
9. *Die Fragmente der Versokratiker*, vol. 1, ed. H. Diels and W. Kranz (Berlin: Wiedmann, 1952).
10. Alexandre Koyré, *From the Closed World to the Infinite Universe* (New York: Johns Hopkins University Press, 1957).

INDEX